This journal belongs to

_____

_____

_____

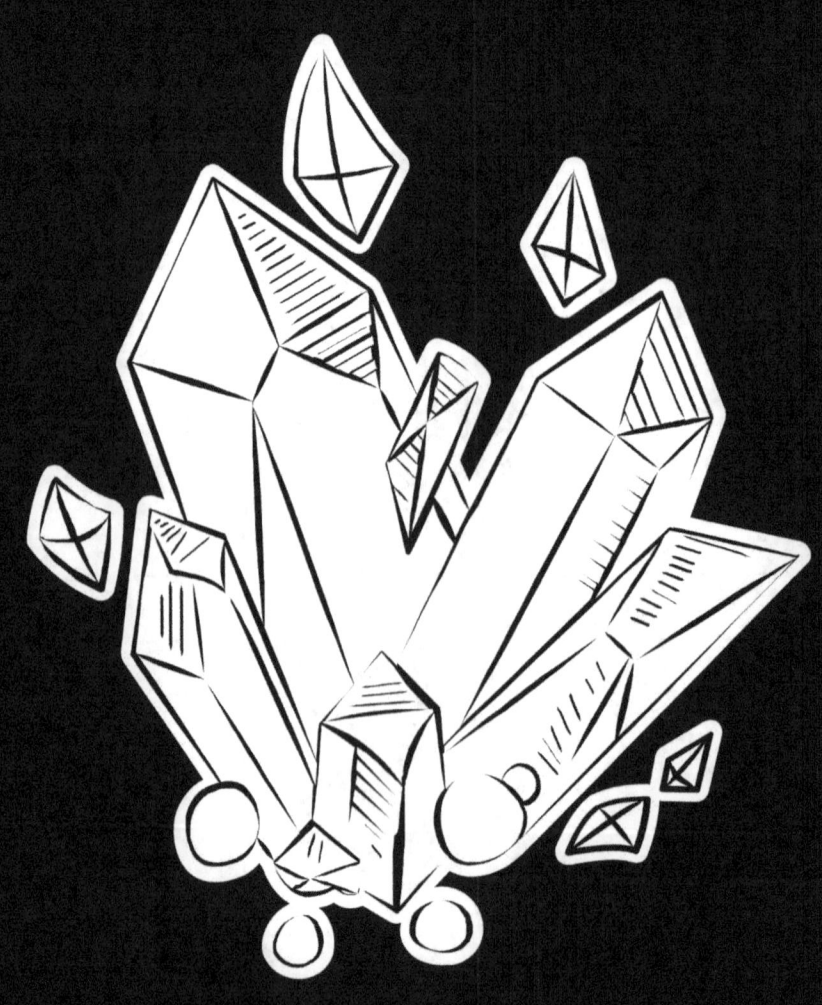

WARLOCKPUBLISHING.COM

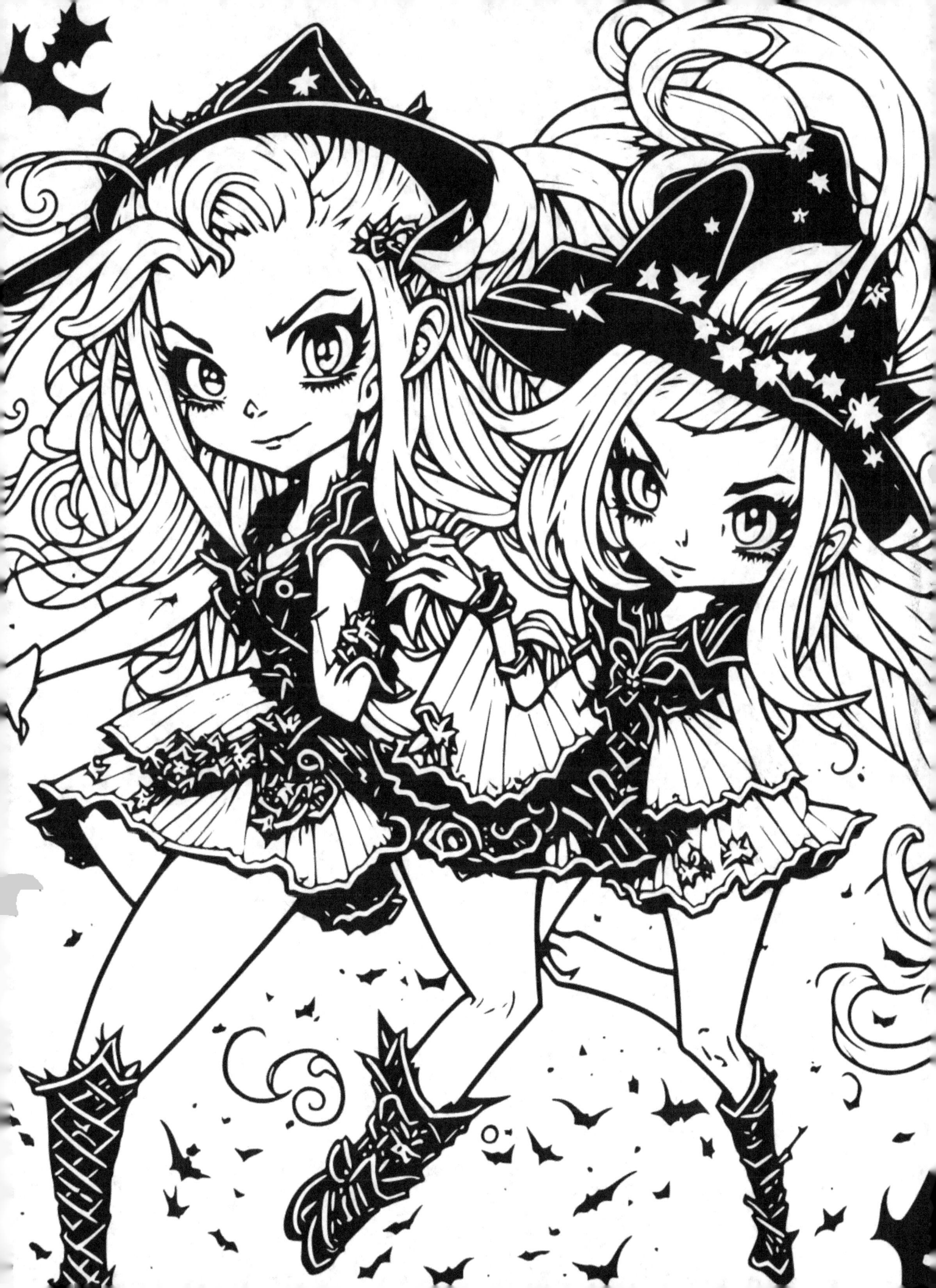

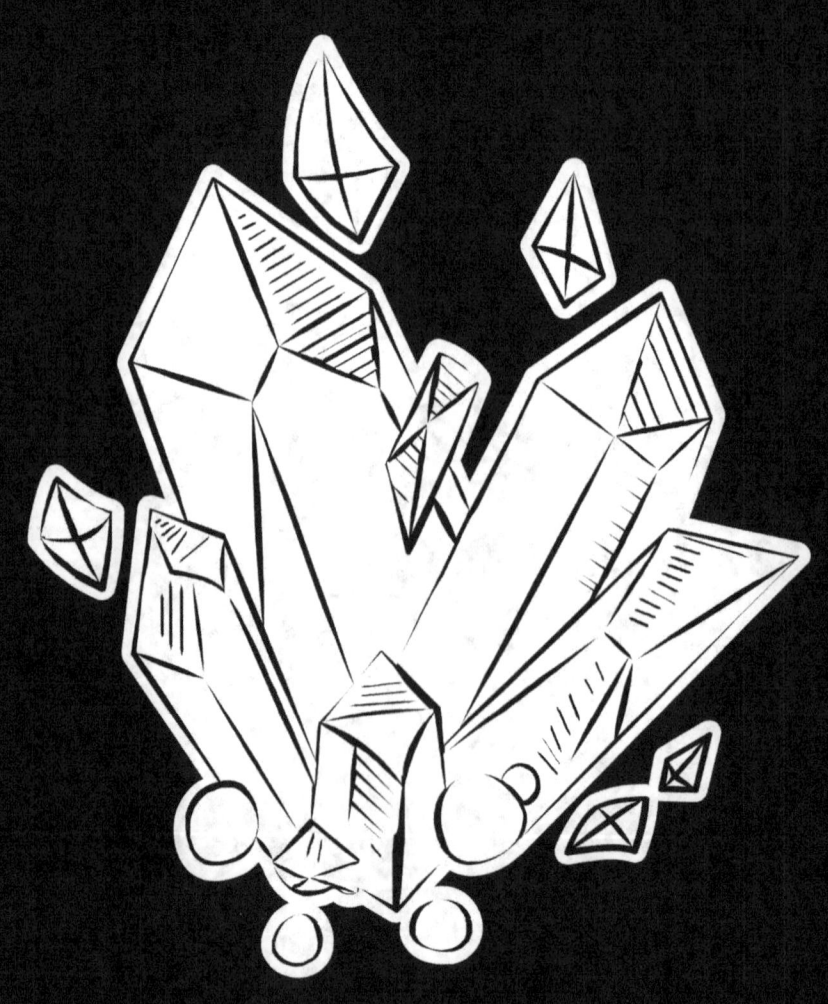

WARLOCKPUBLISHING.COM

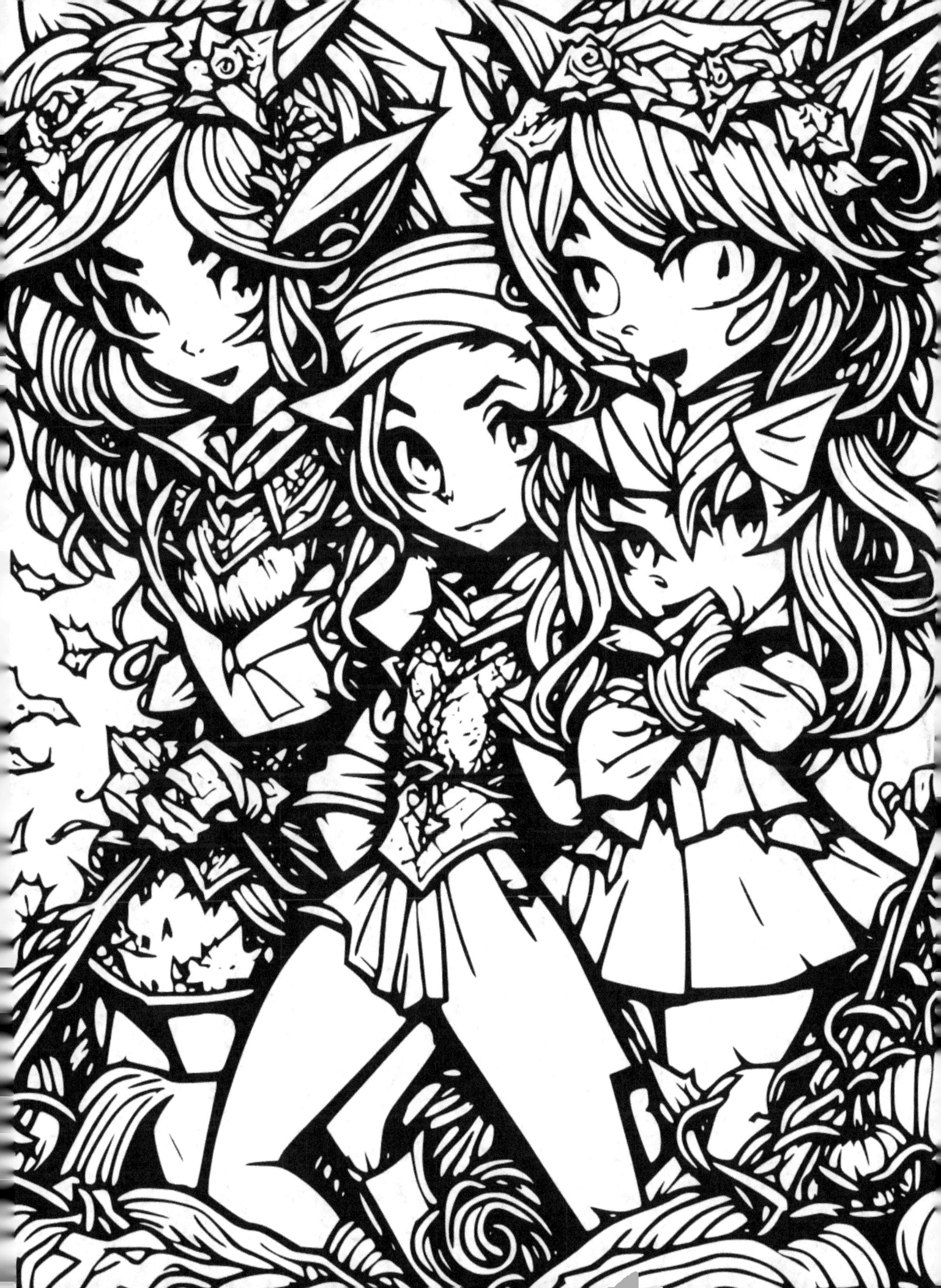

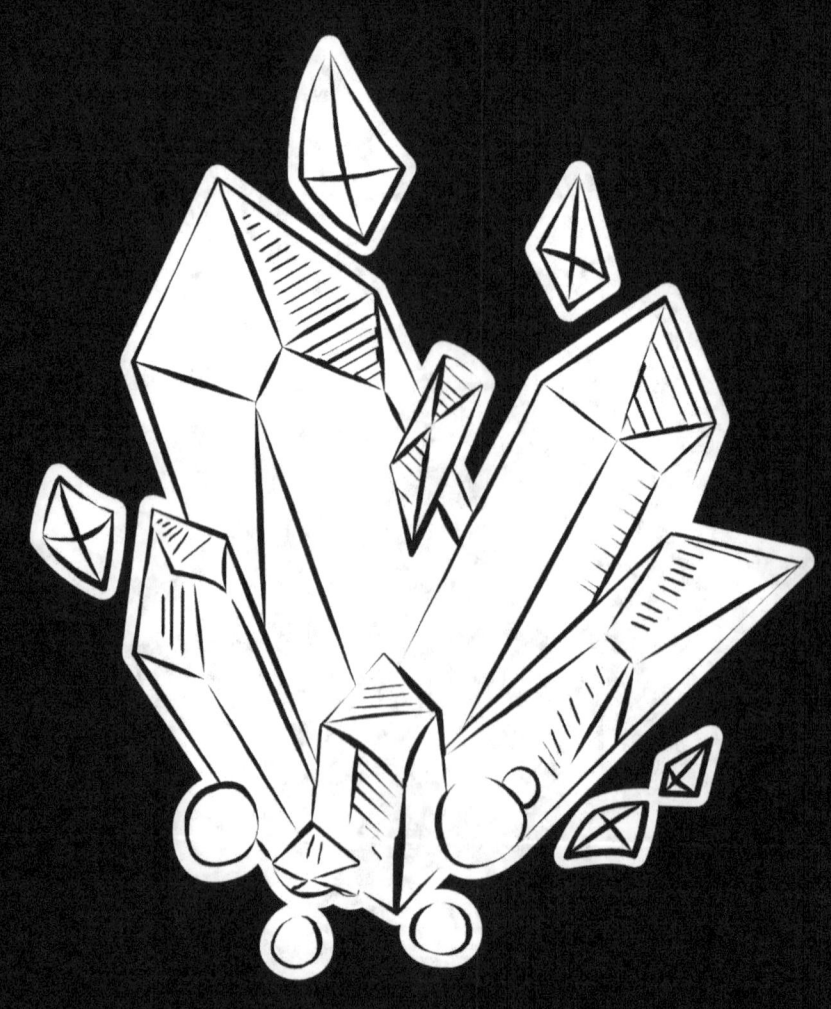

WARLOCKPUBLISHING.COM

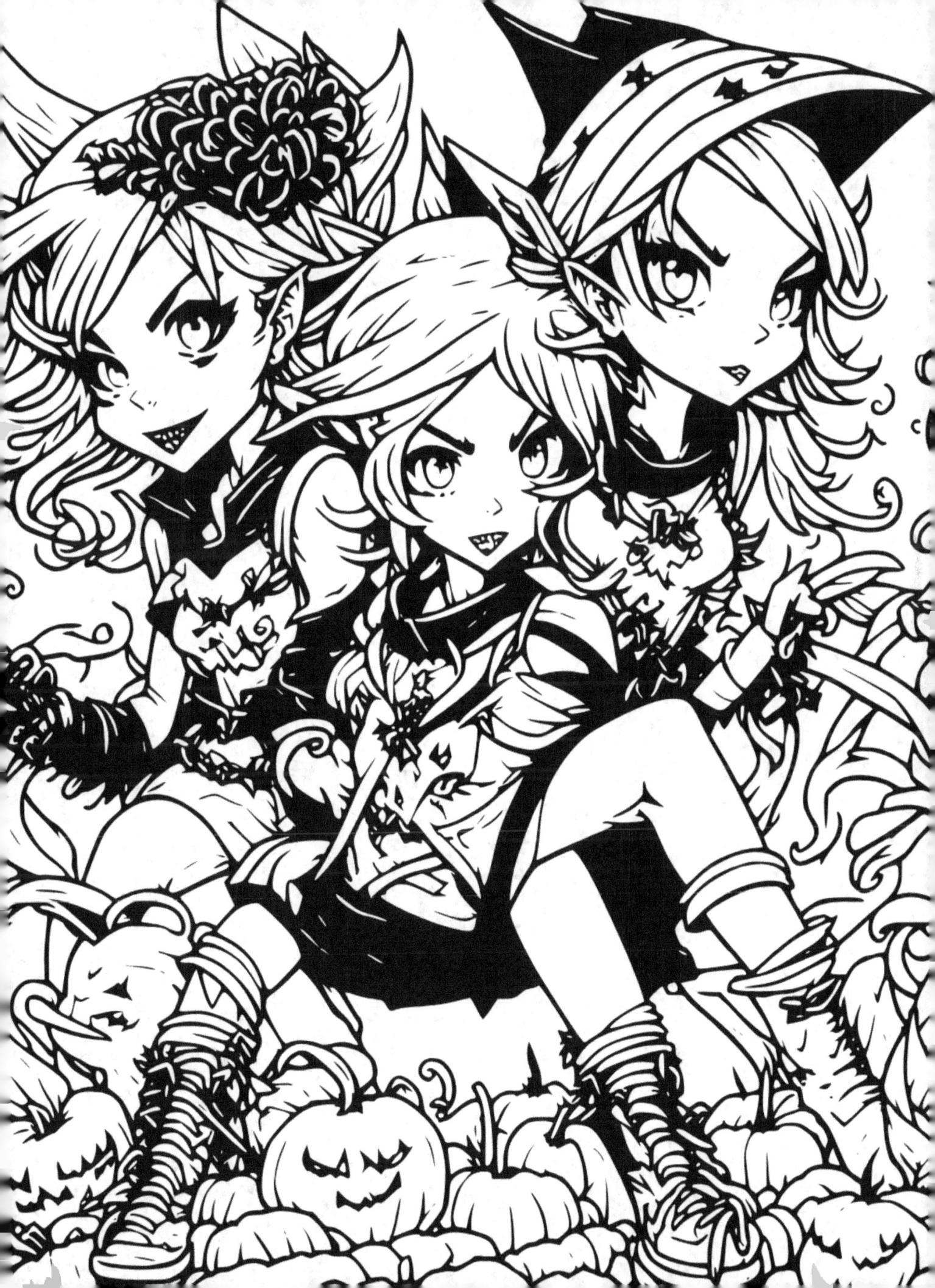

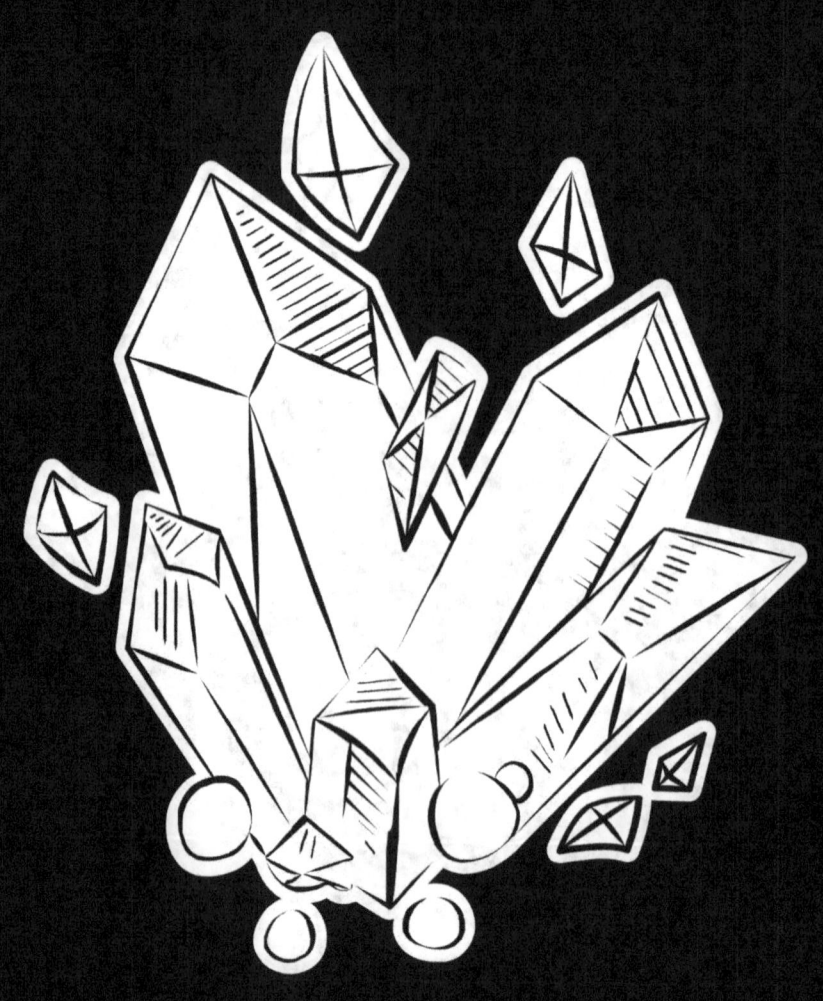

WARLOCKPUBLISHING.COM

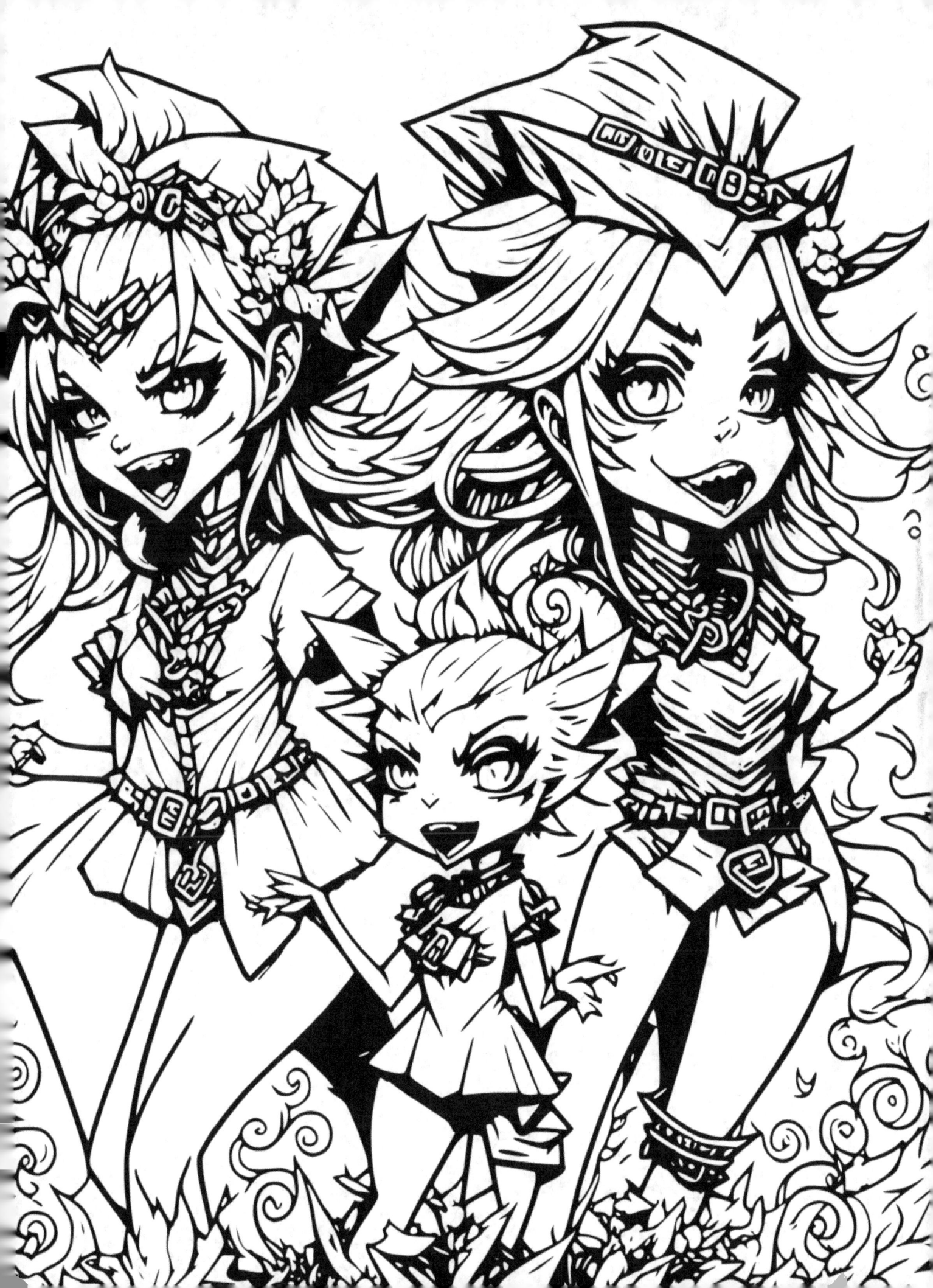

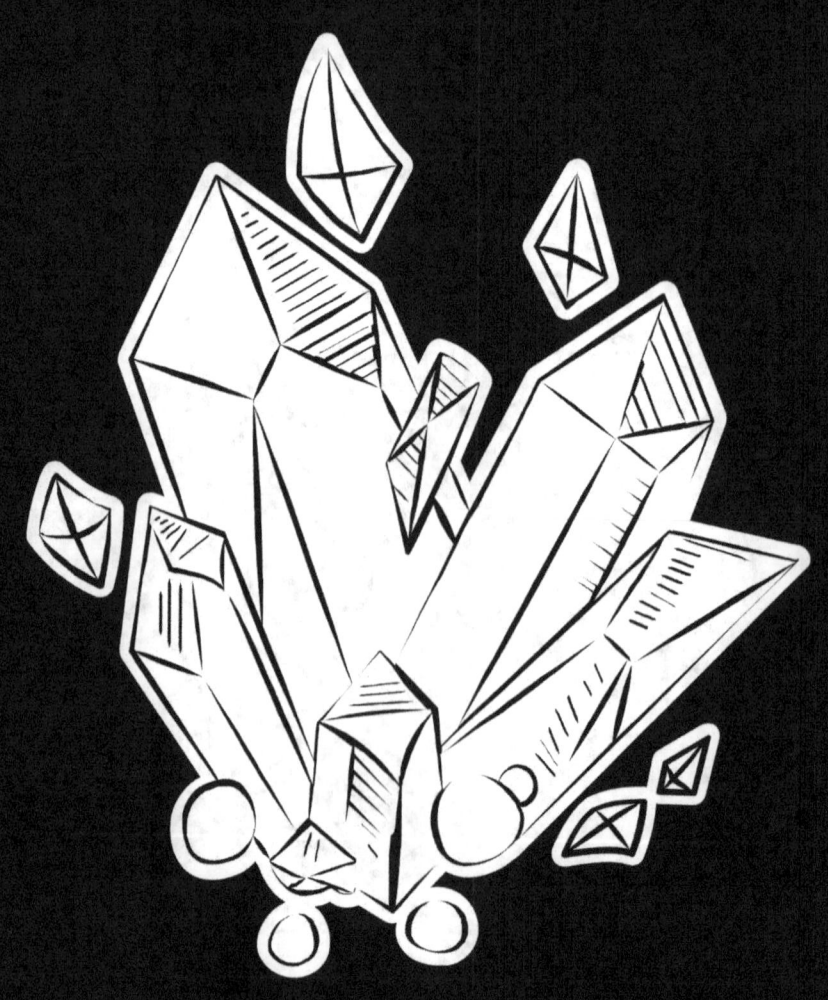

WARLOCKPUBLISHING.COM

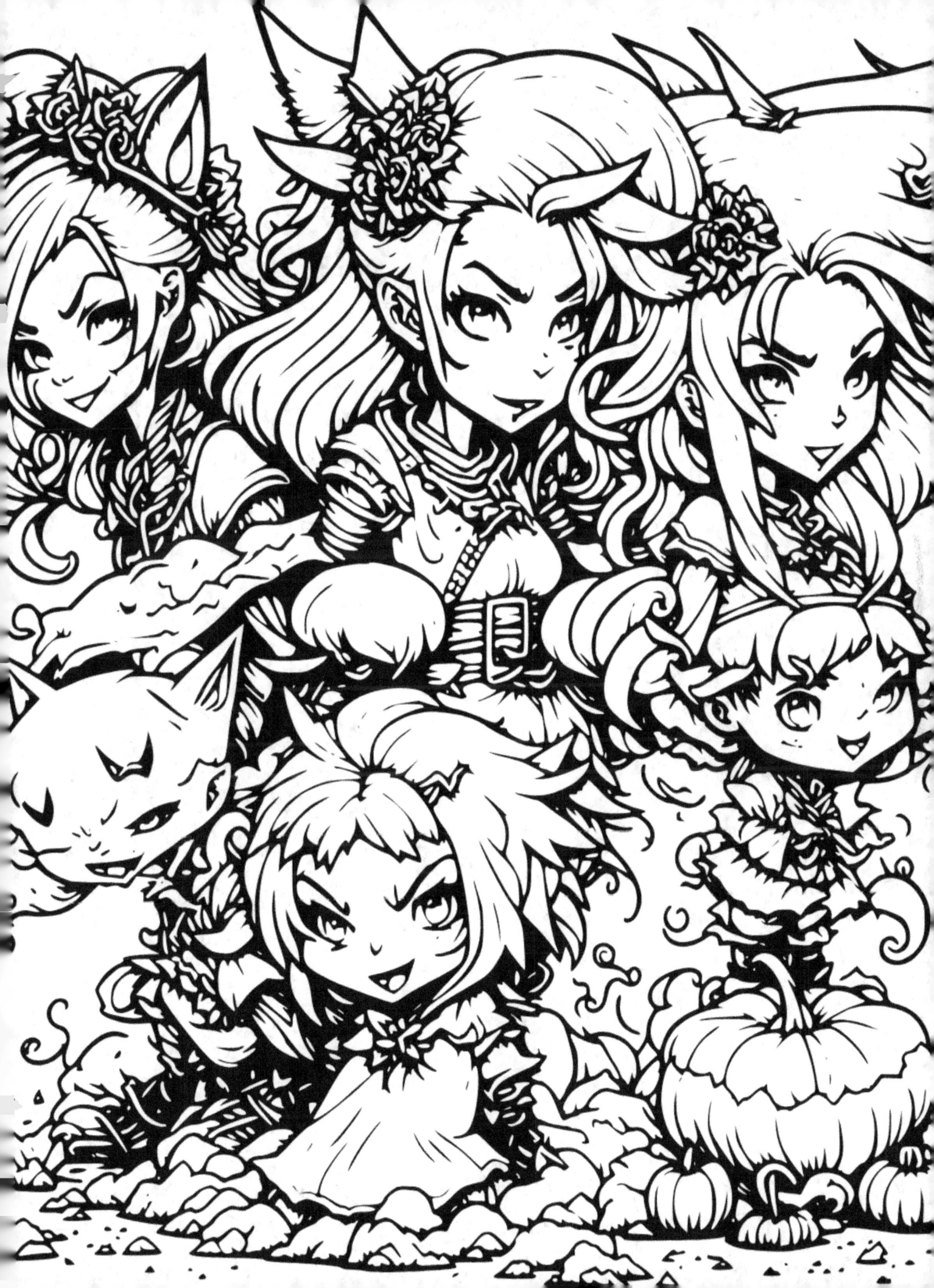

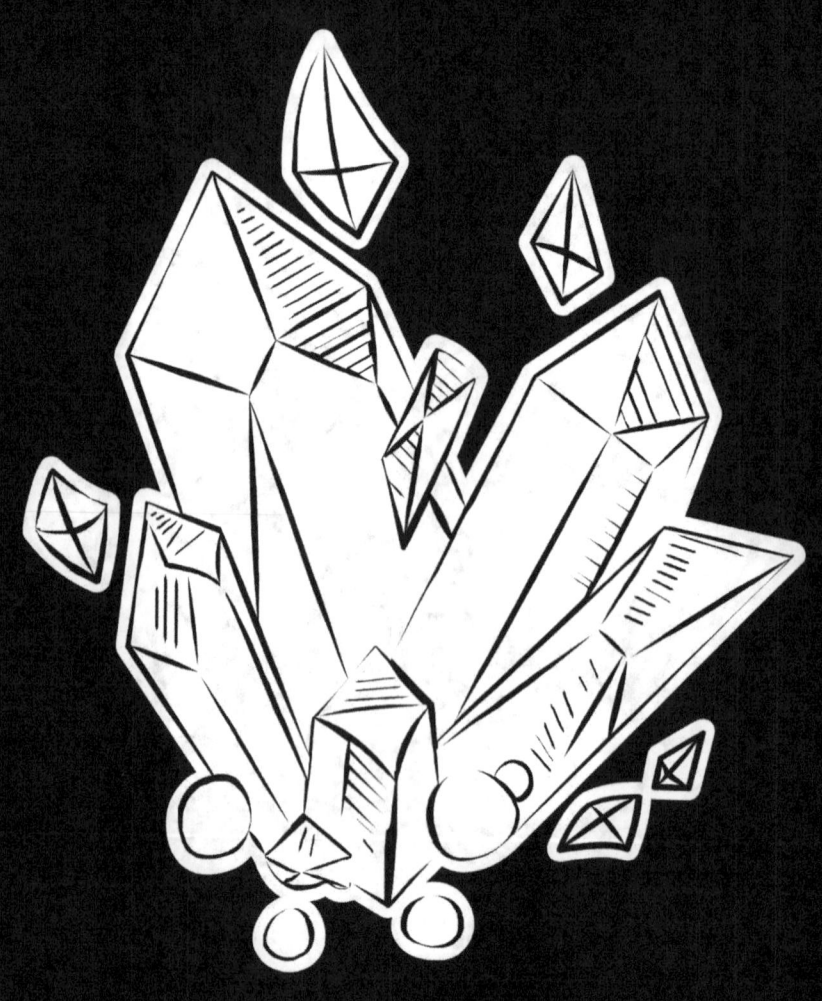

WARLOCKPUBLISHING.COM

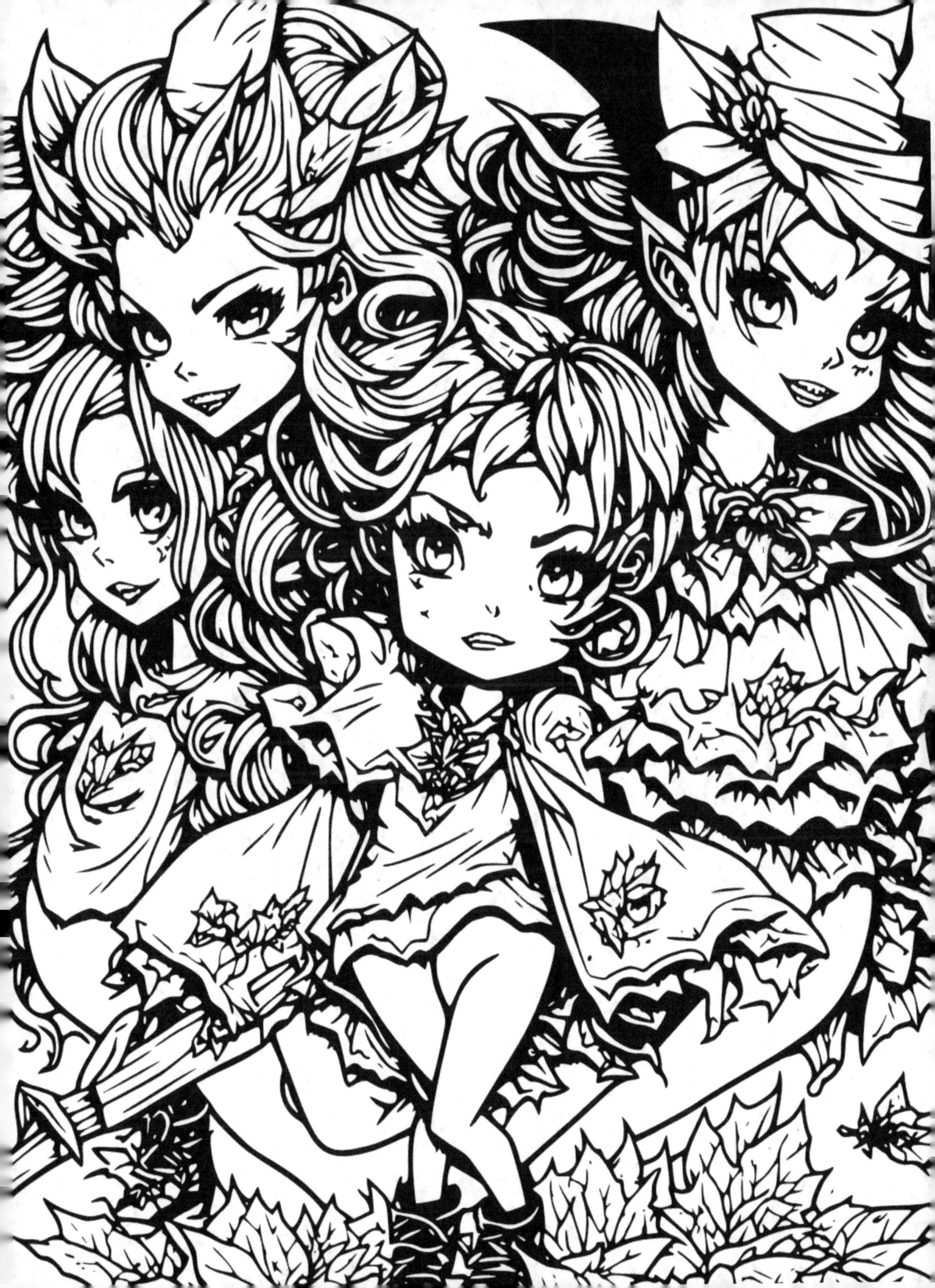

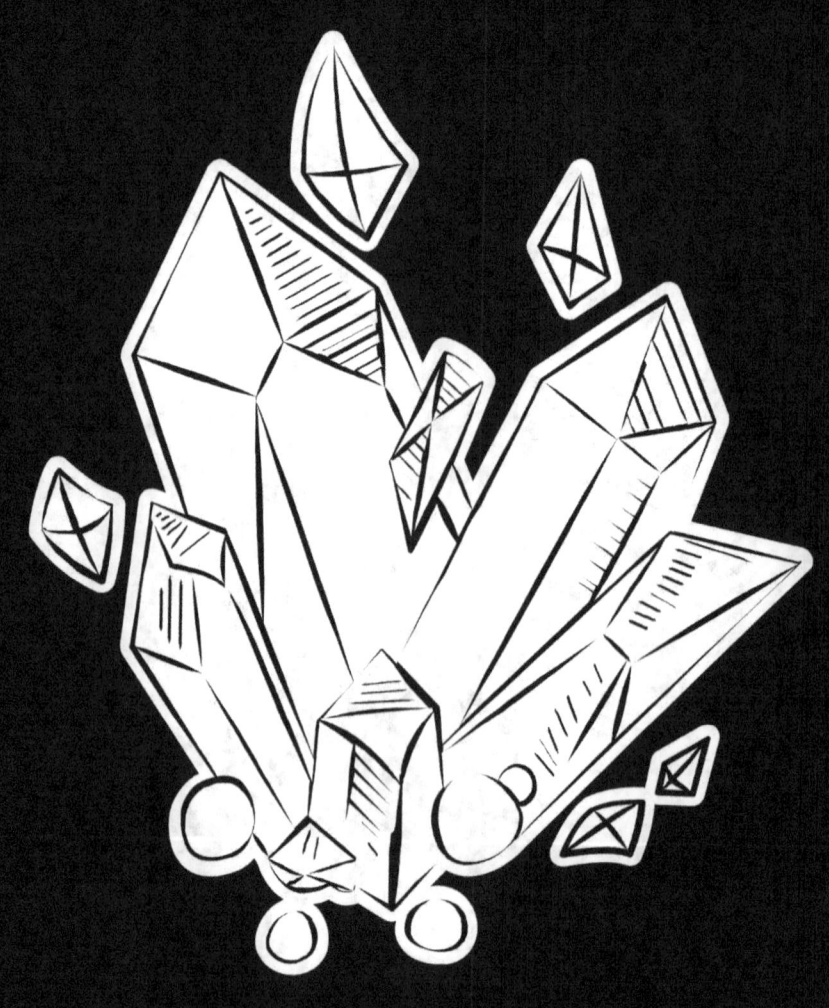

WARLOCKPUBLISHING.COM

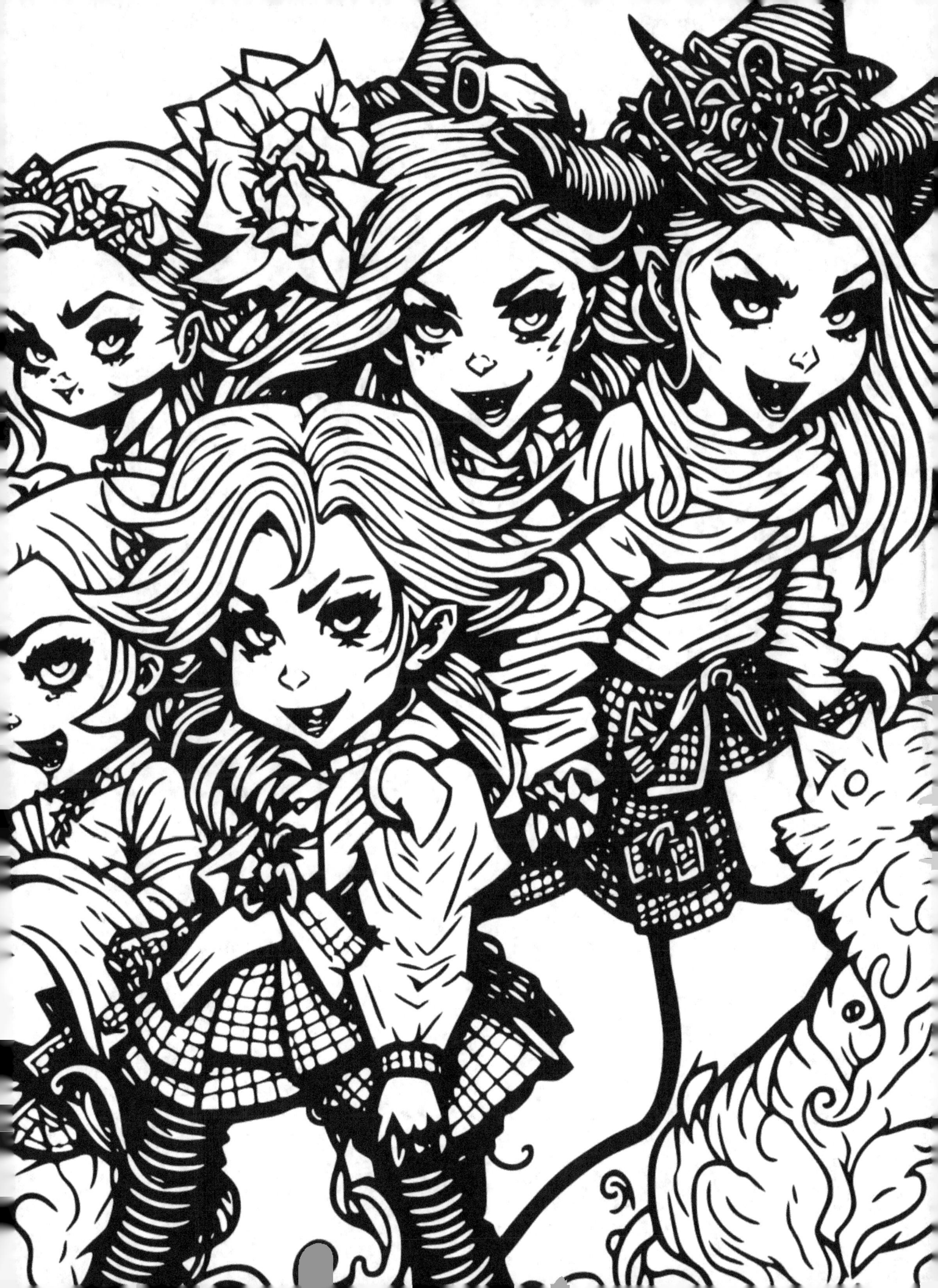

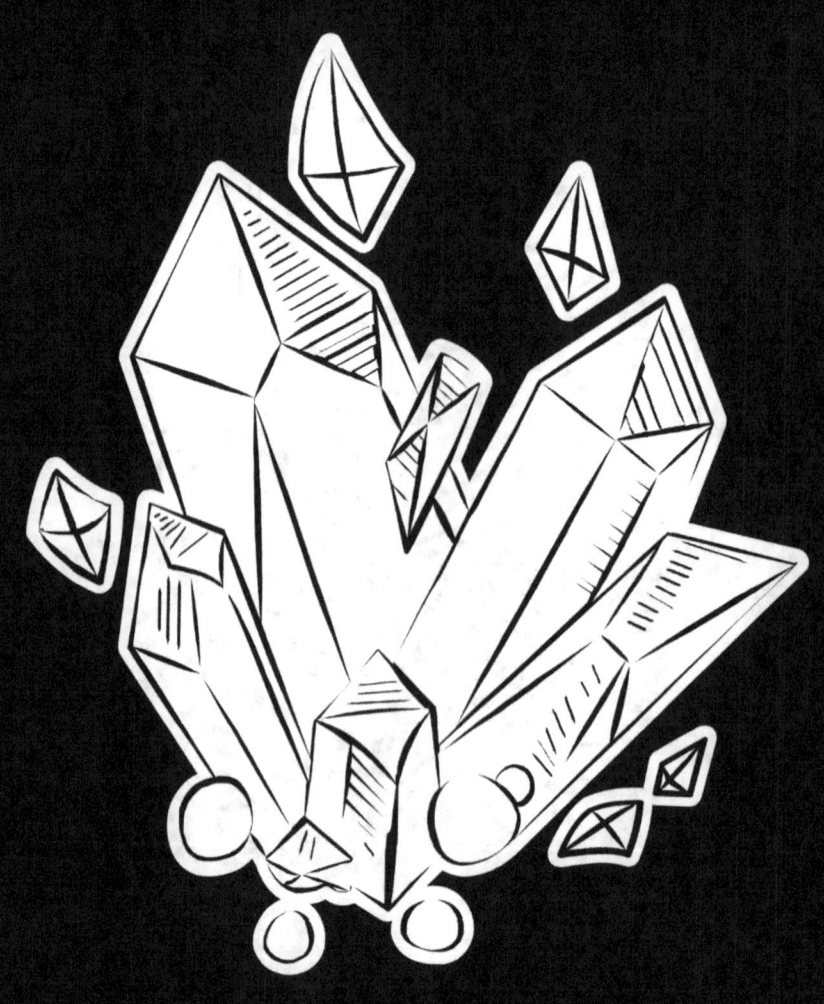

WARLOCKPUBLISHING.COM

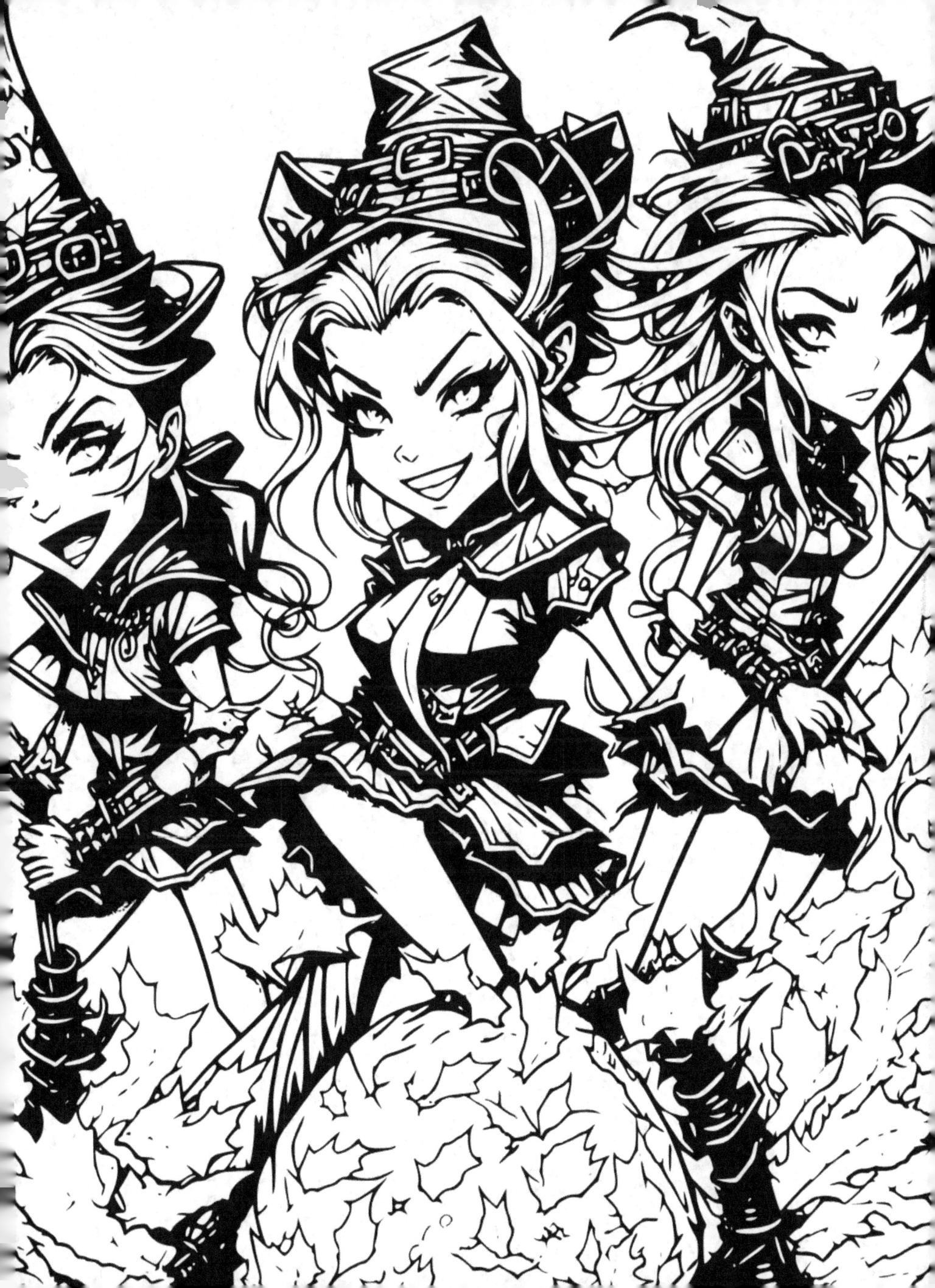

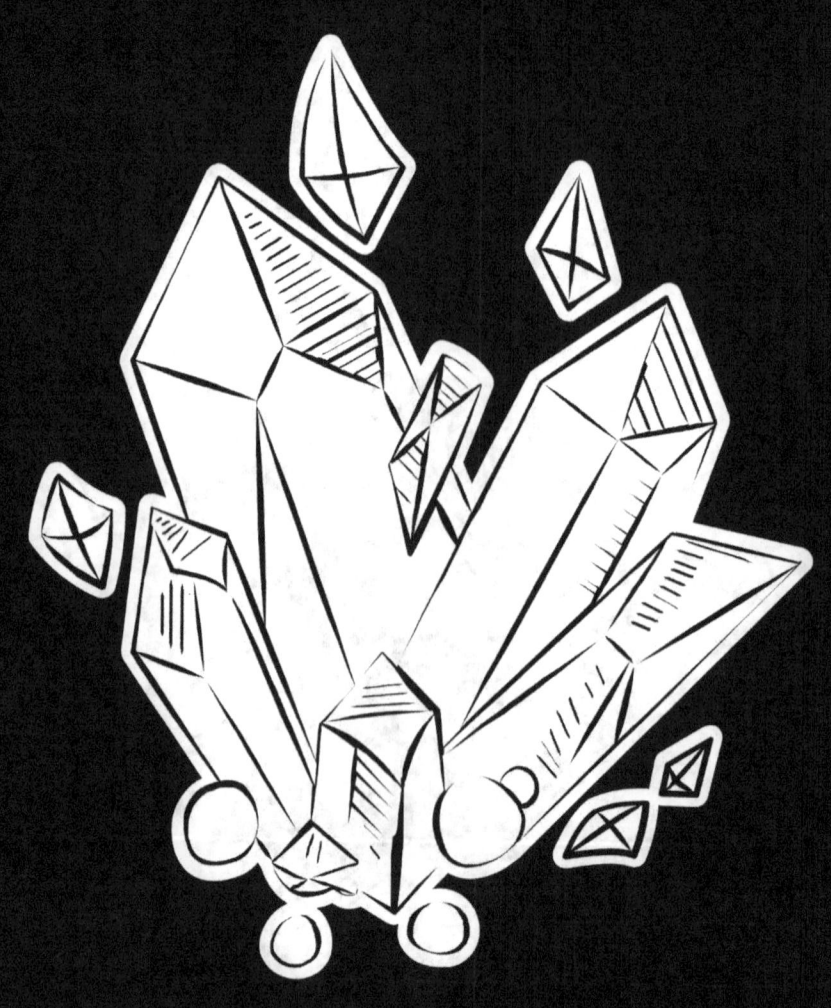

WARLOCKPUBLISHING.COM

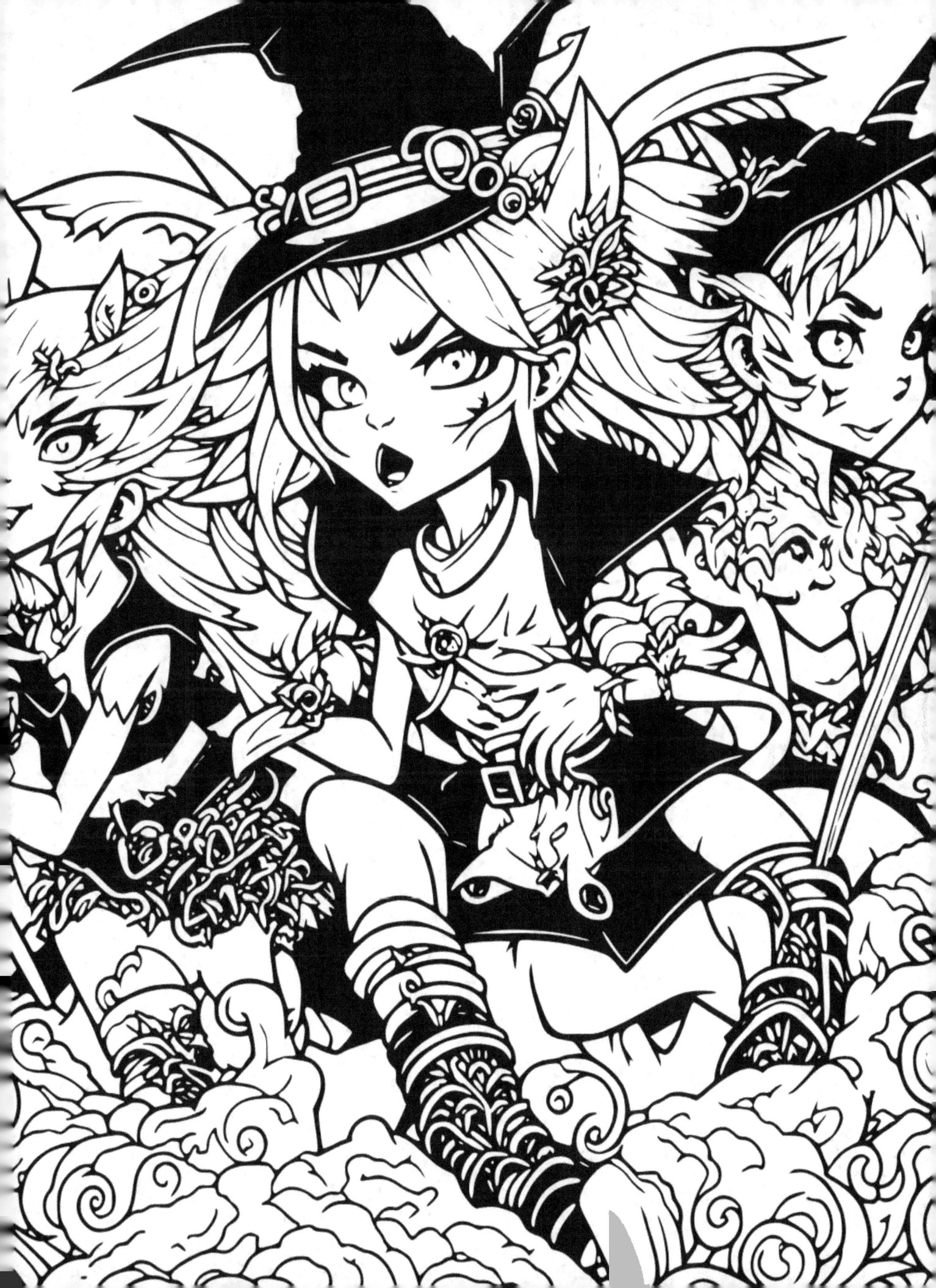

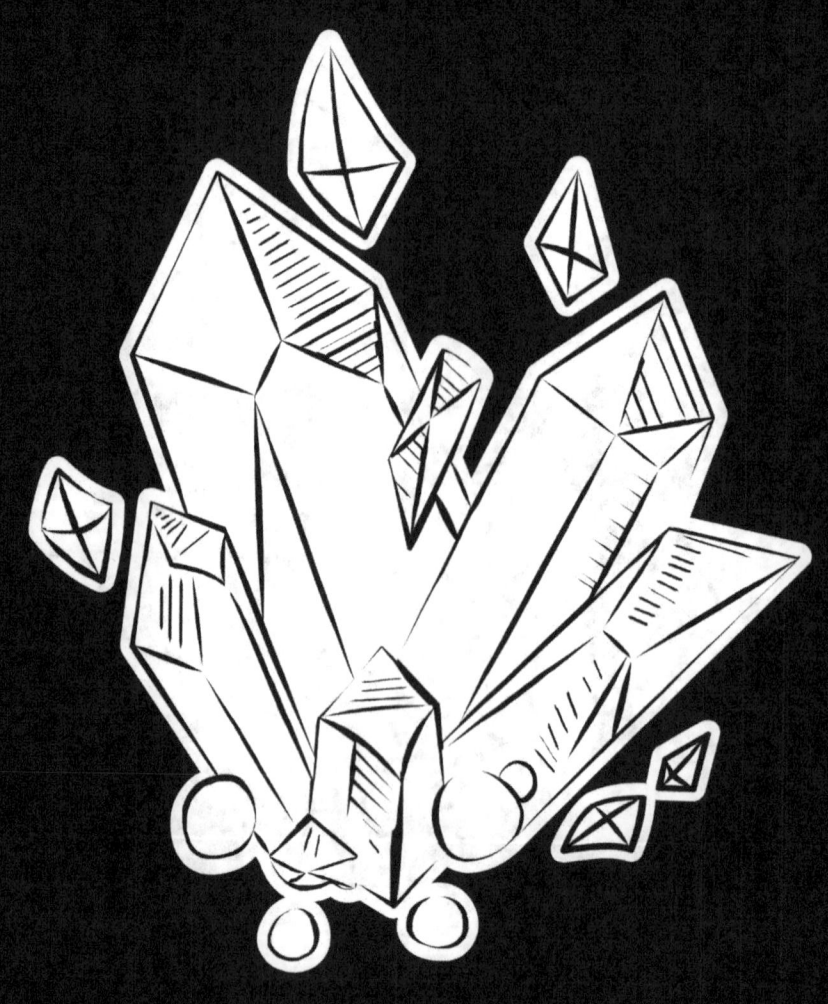

WARLOCKPUBLISHING.COM

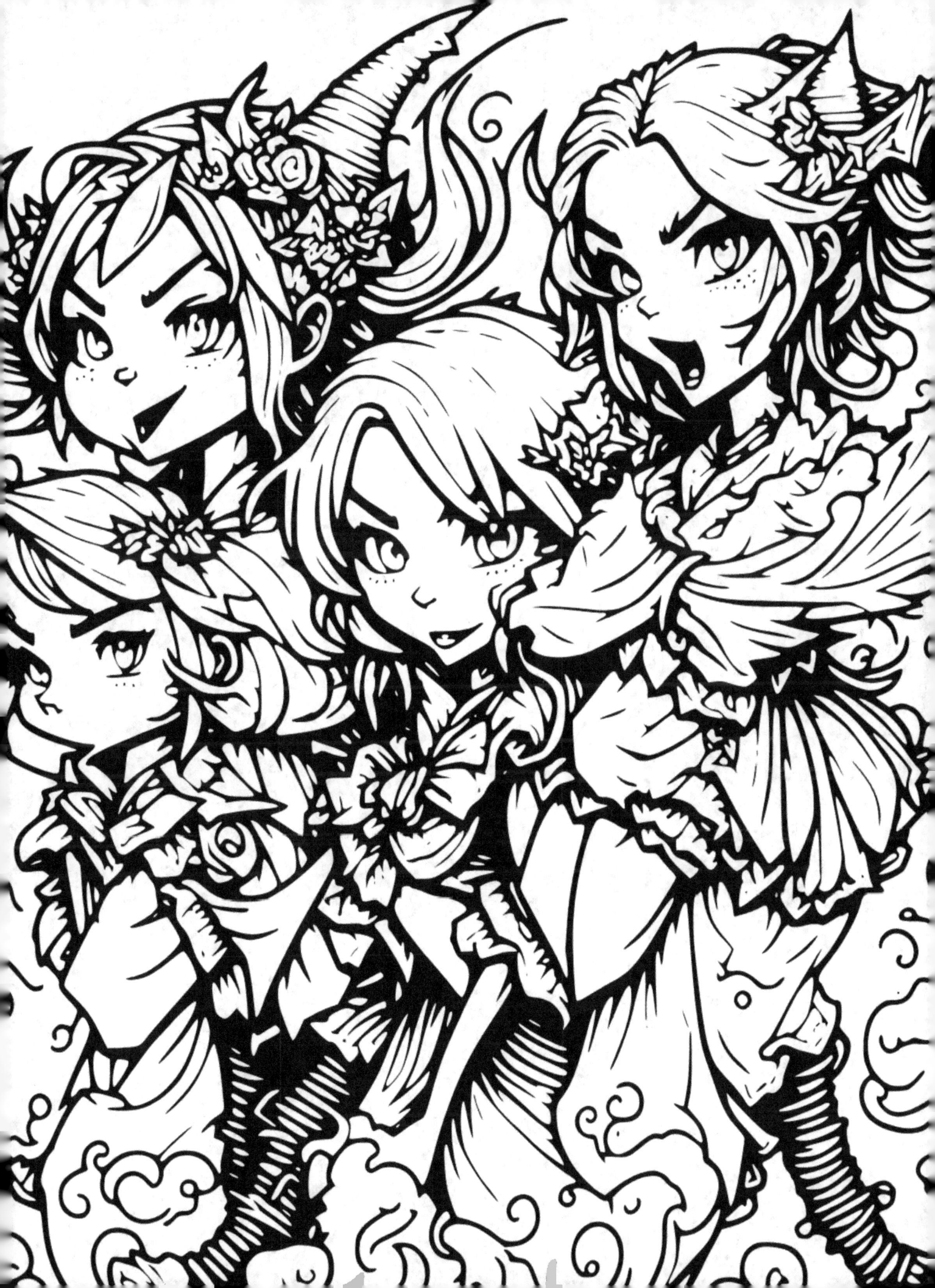

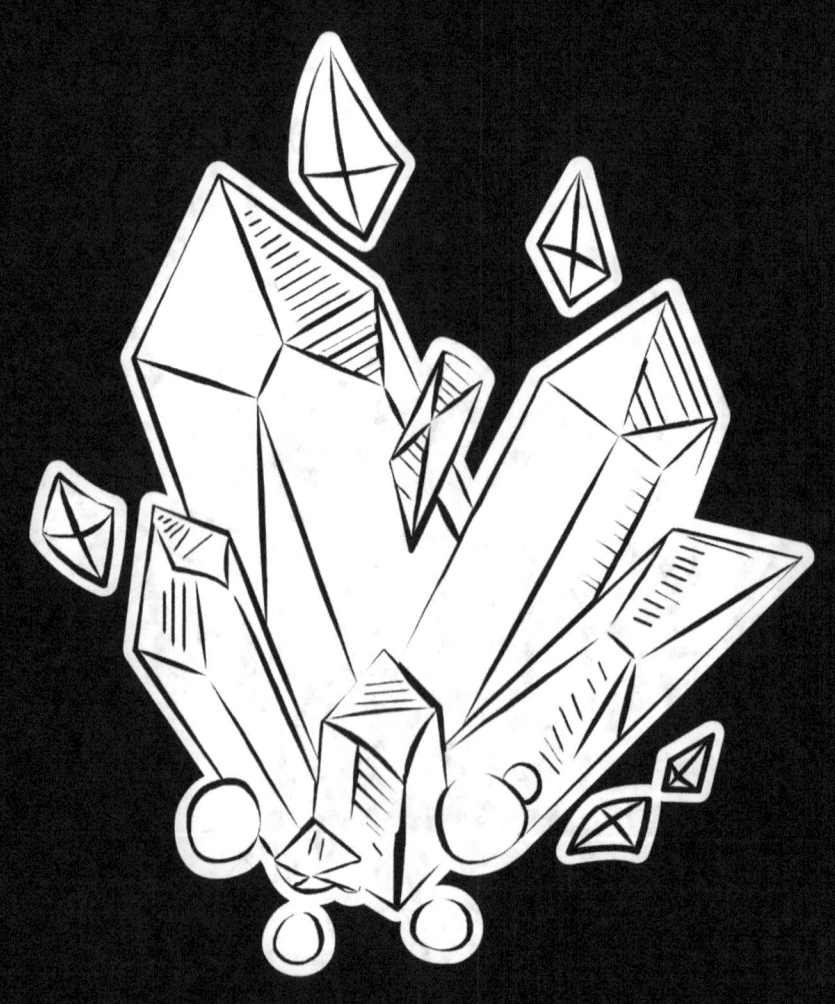

WARLOCKPUBLISHING.COM

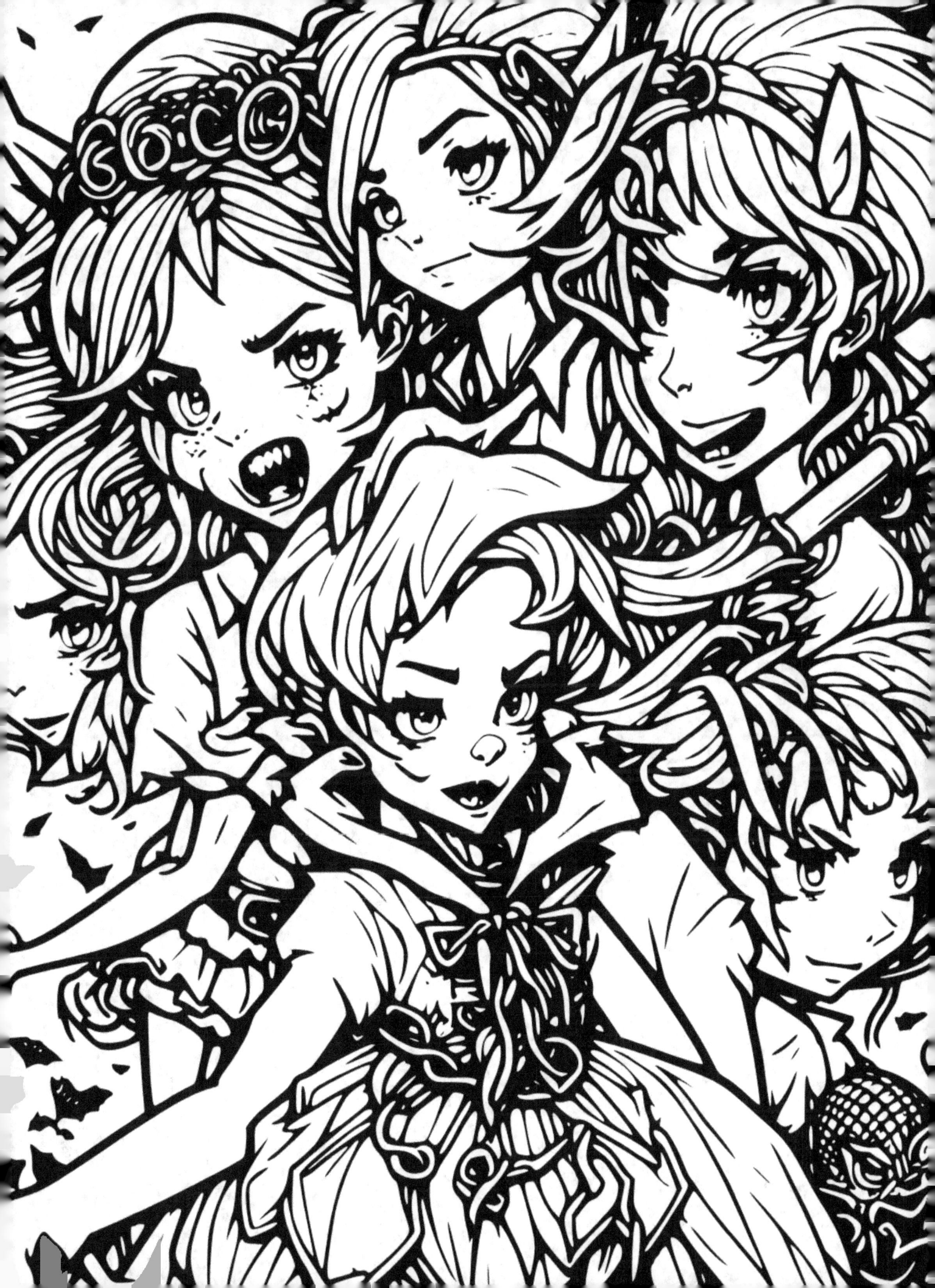

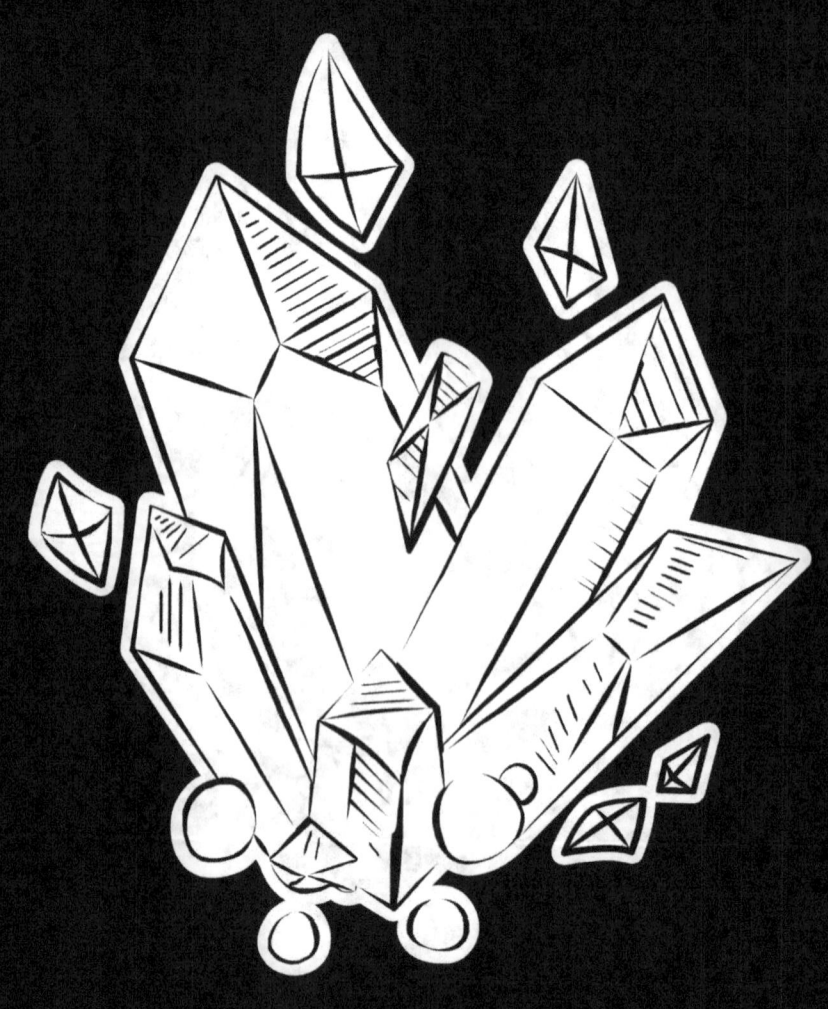

WARLOCKPUBLISHING.COM

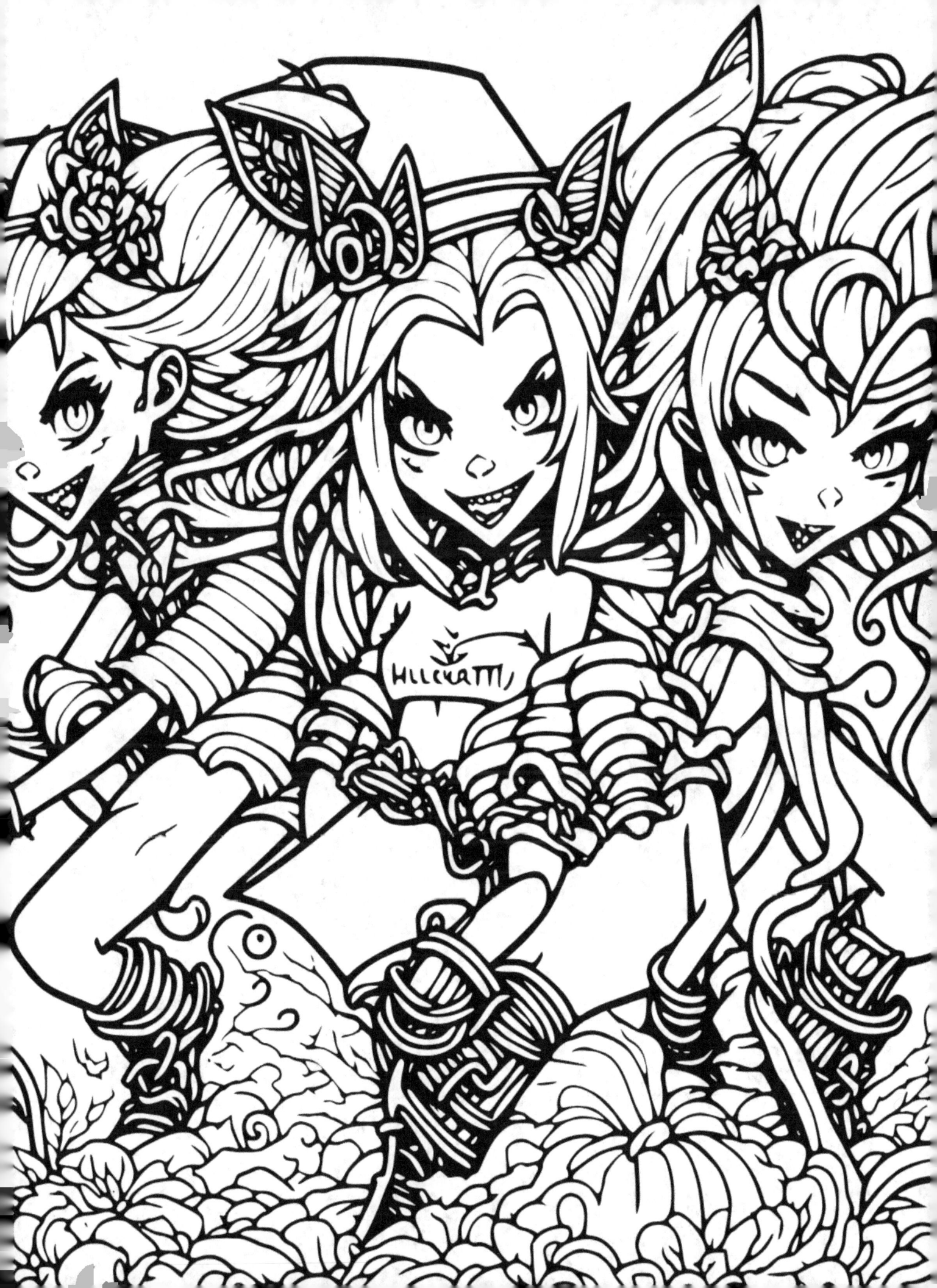

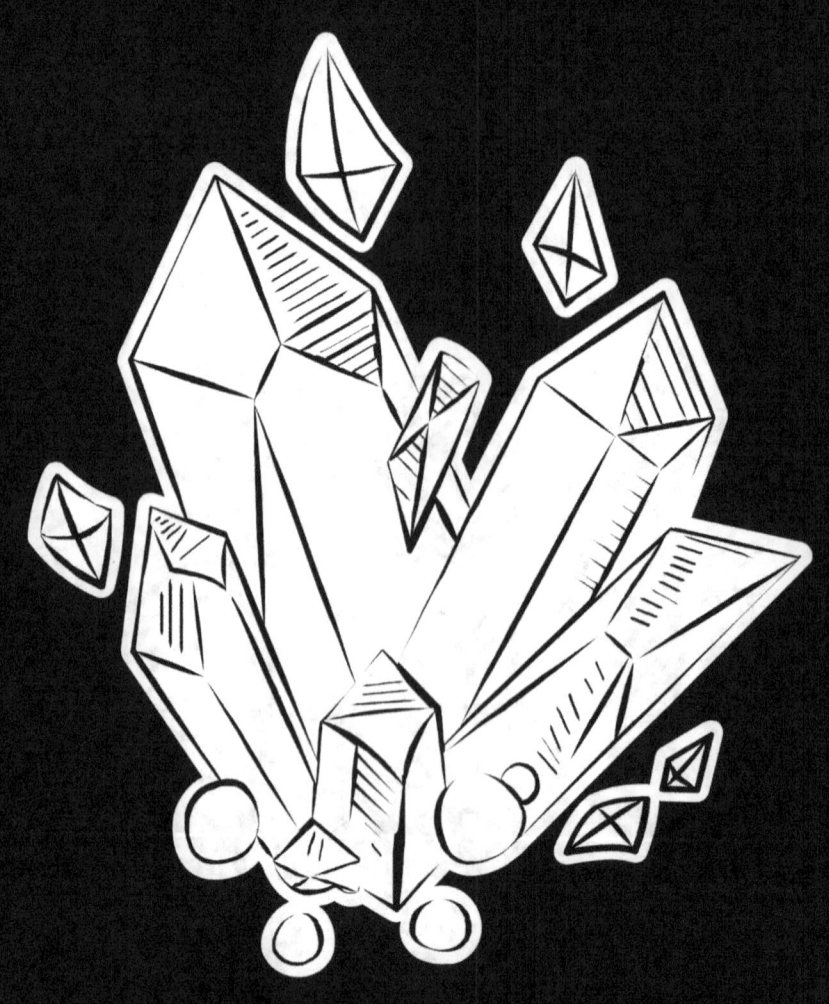

WARLOCKPUBLISHING.COM

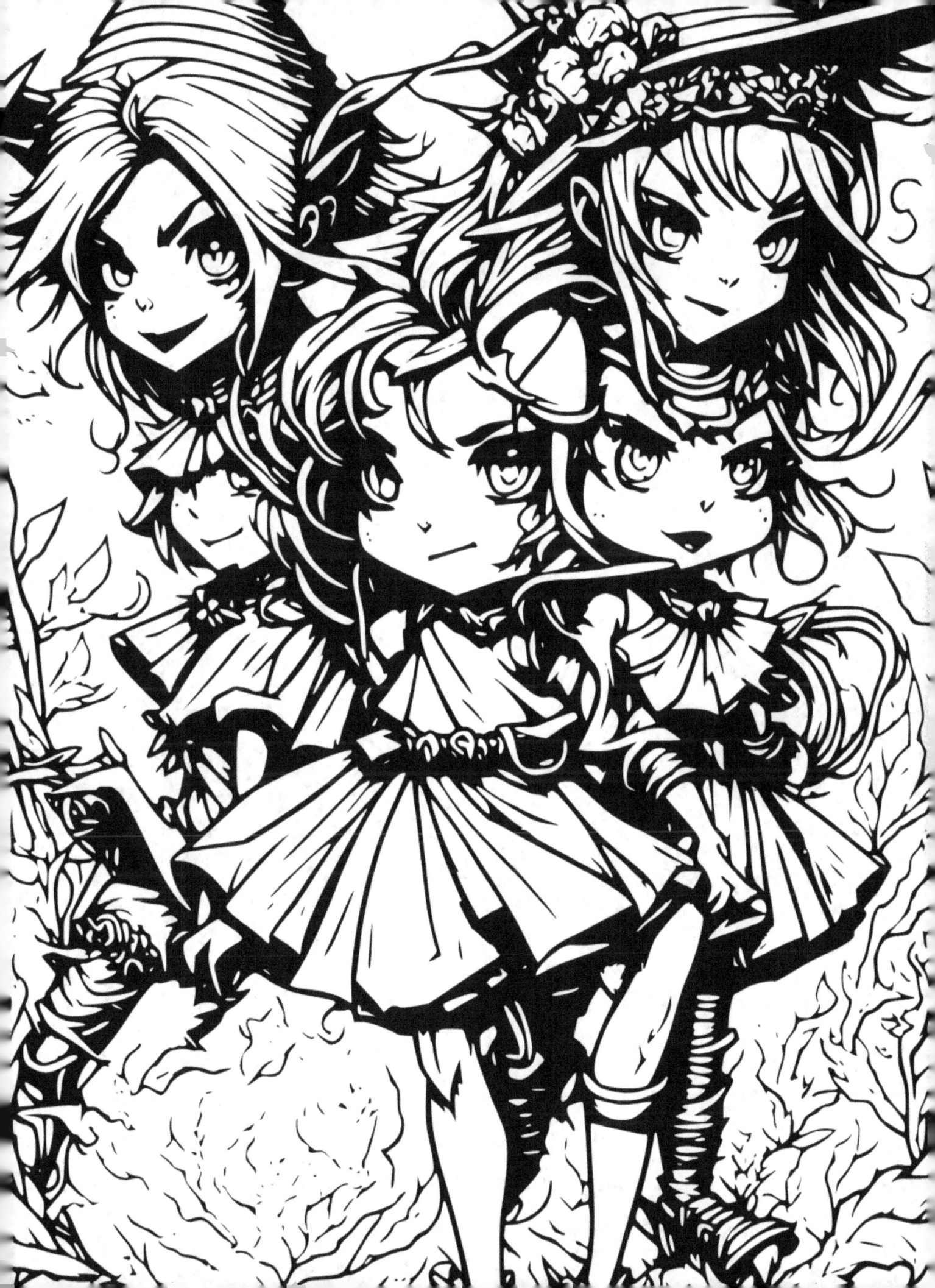

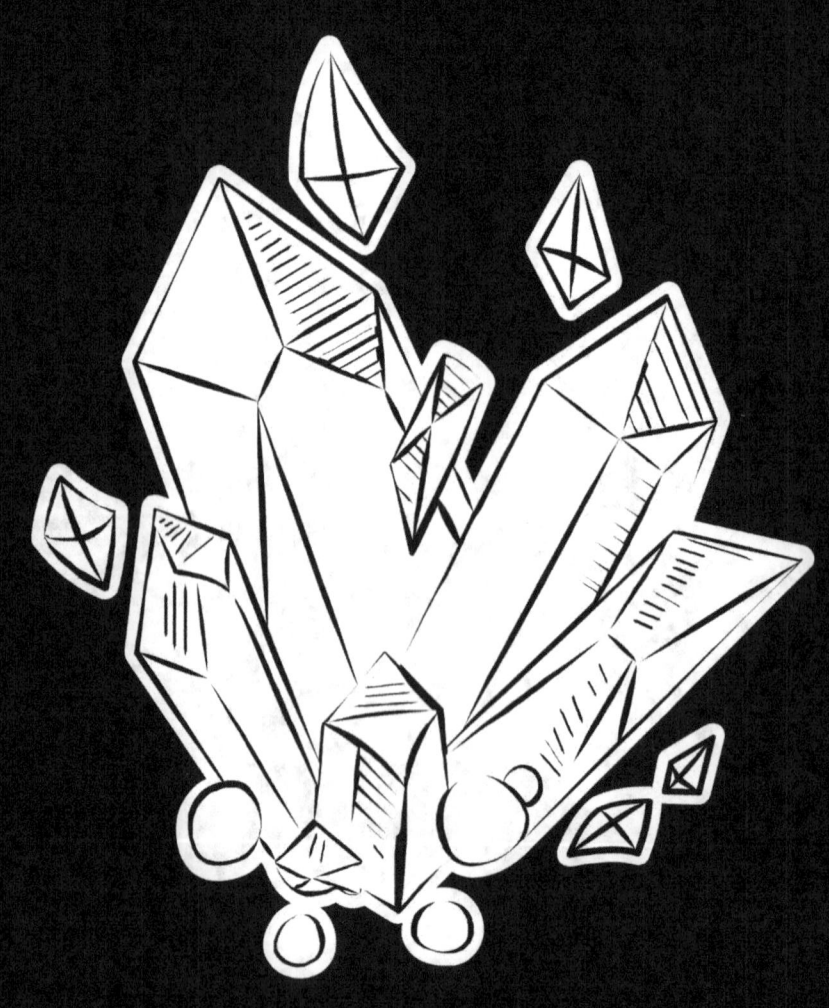

WARLOCKPUBLISHING.COM

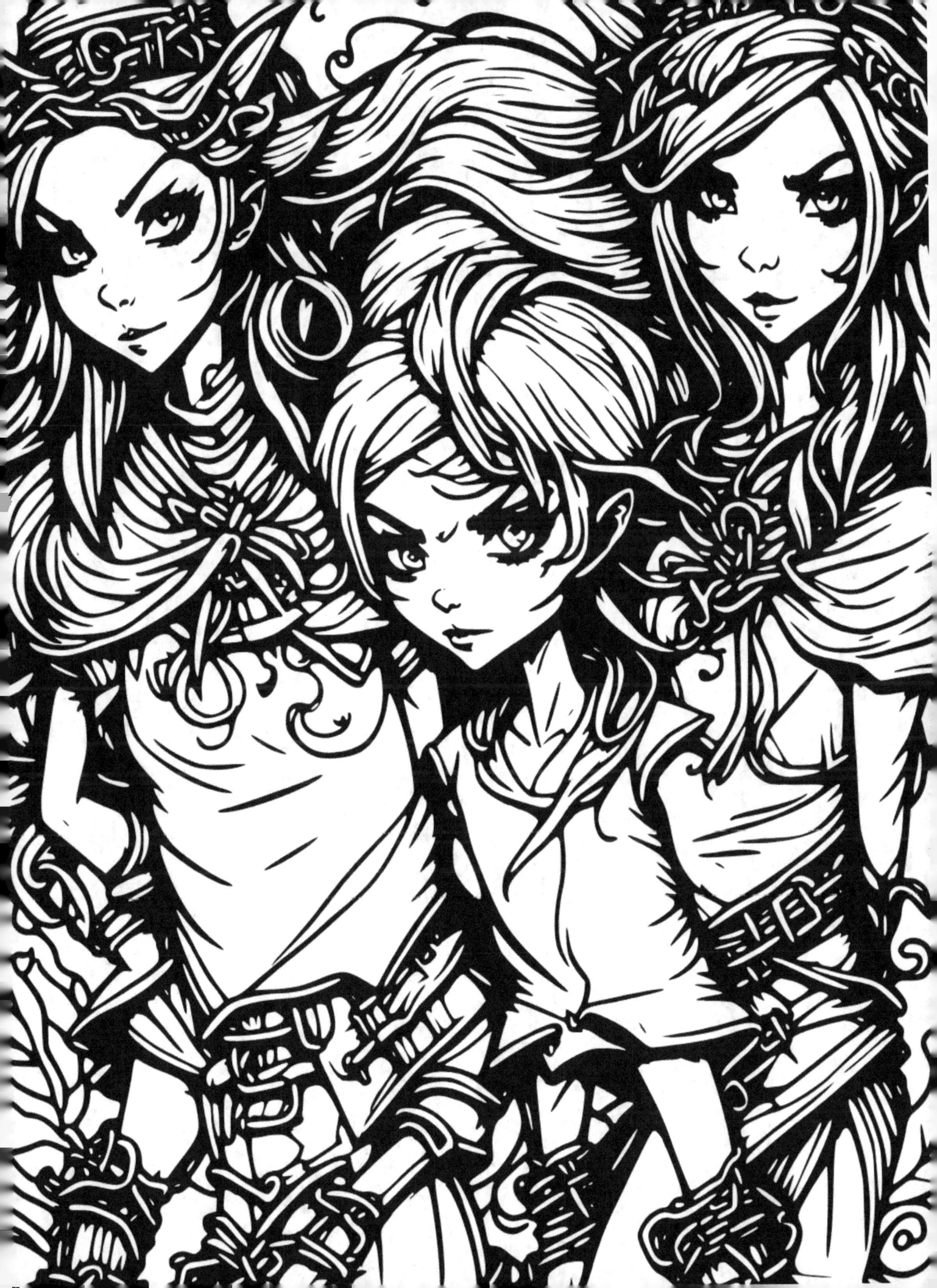

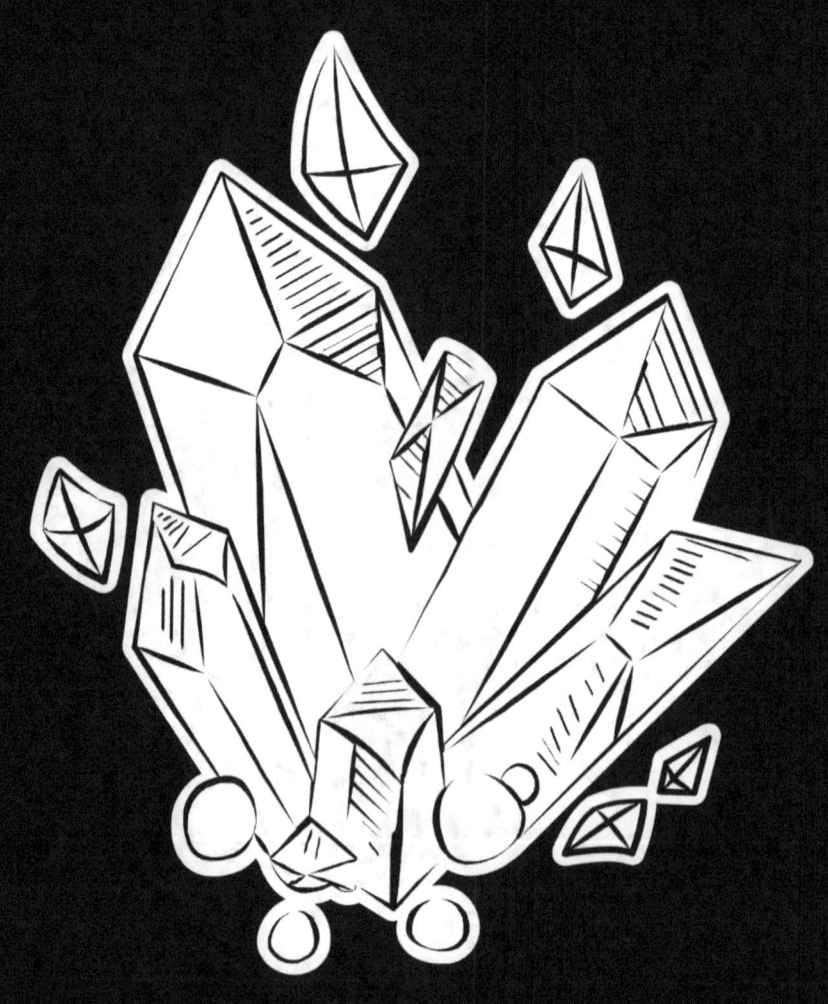

WARLOCKPUBLISHING.COM

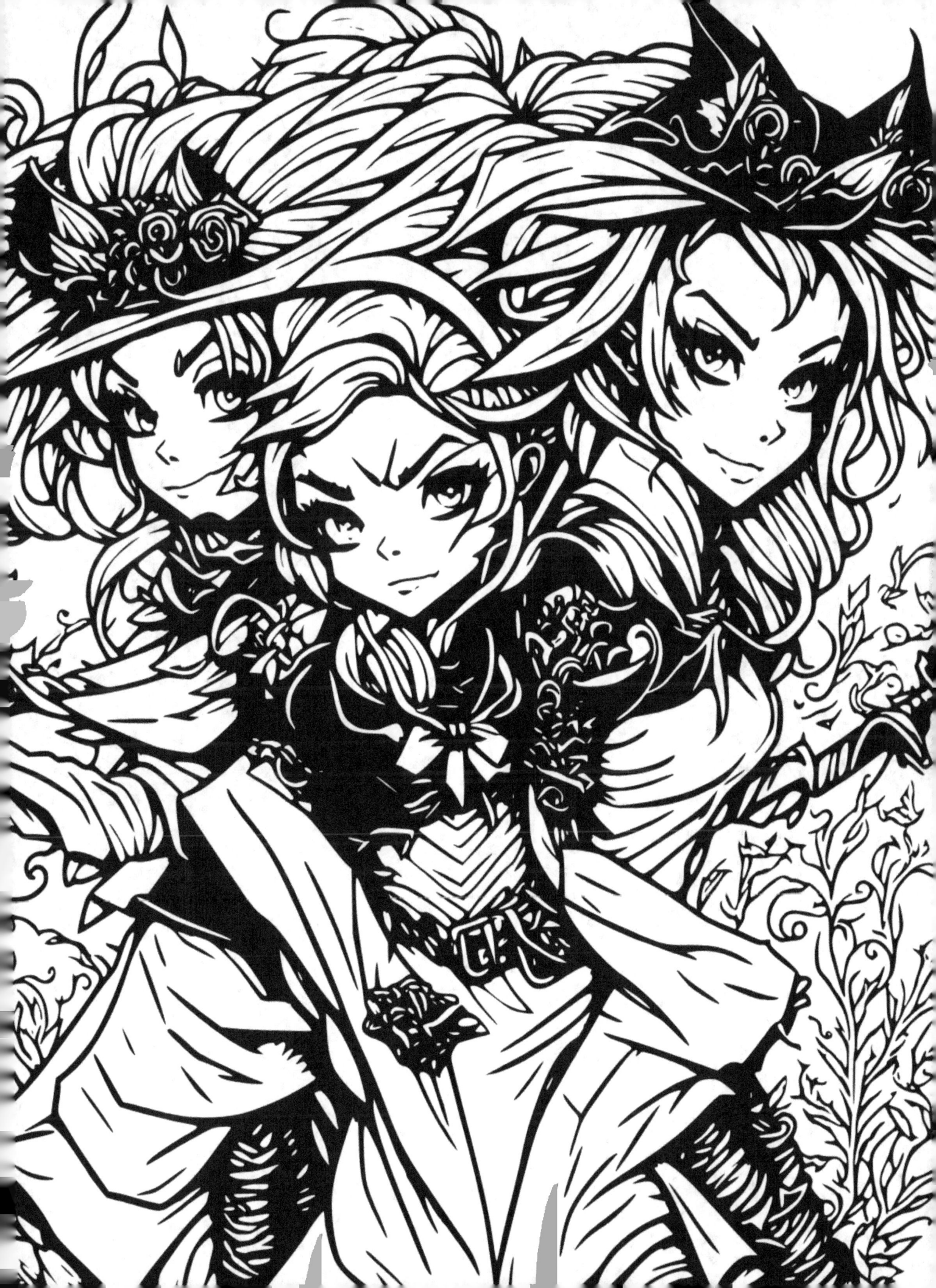

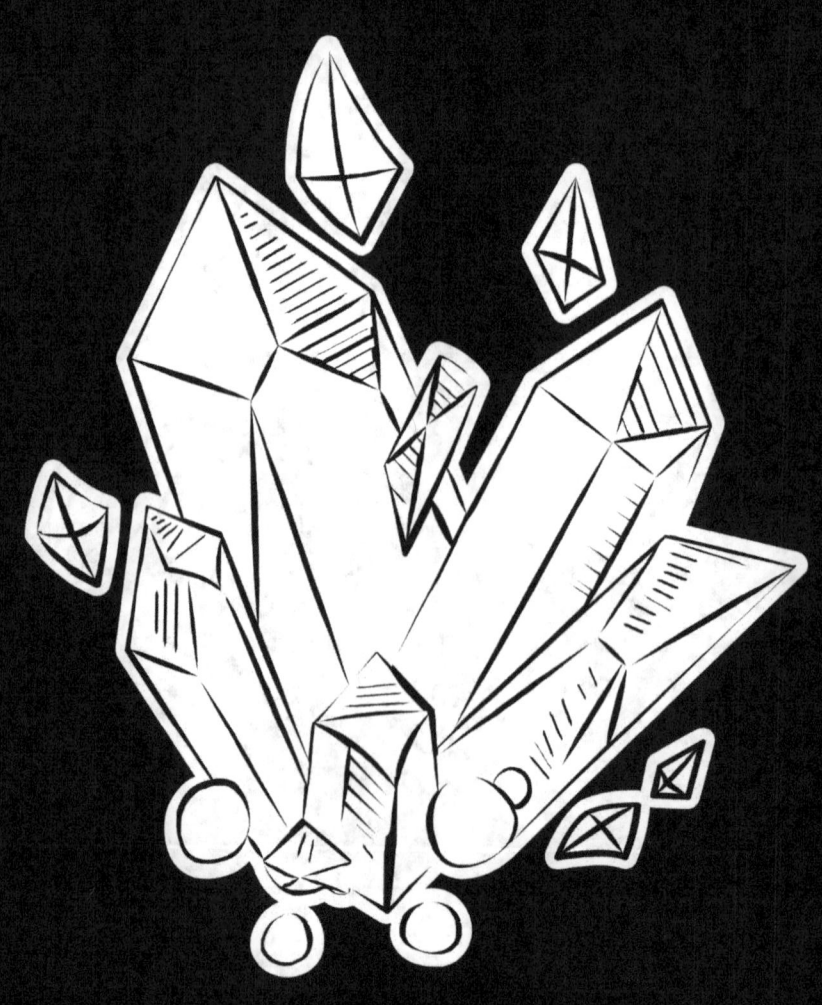

WARLOCKPUBLISHING.COM

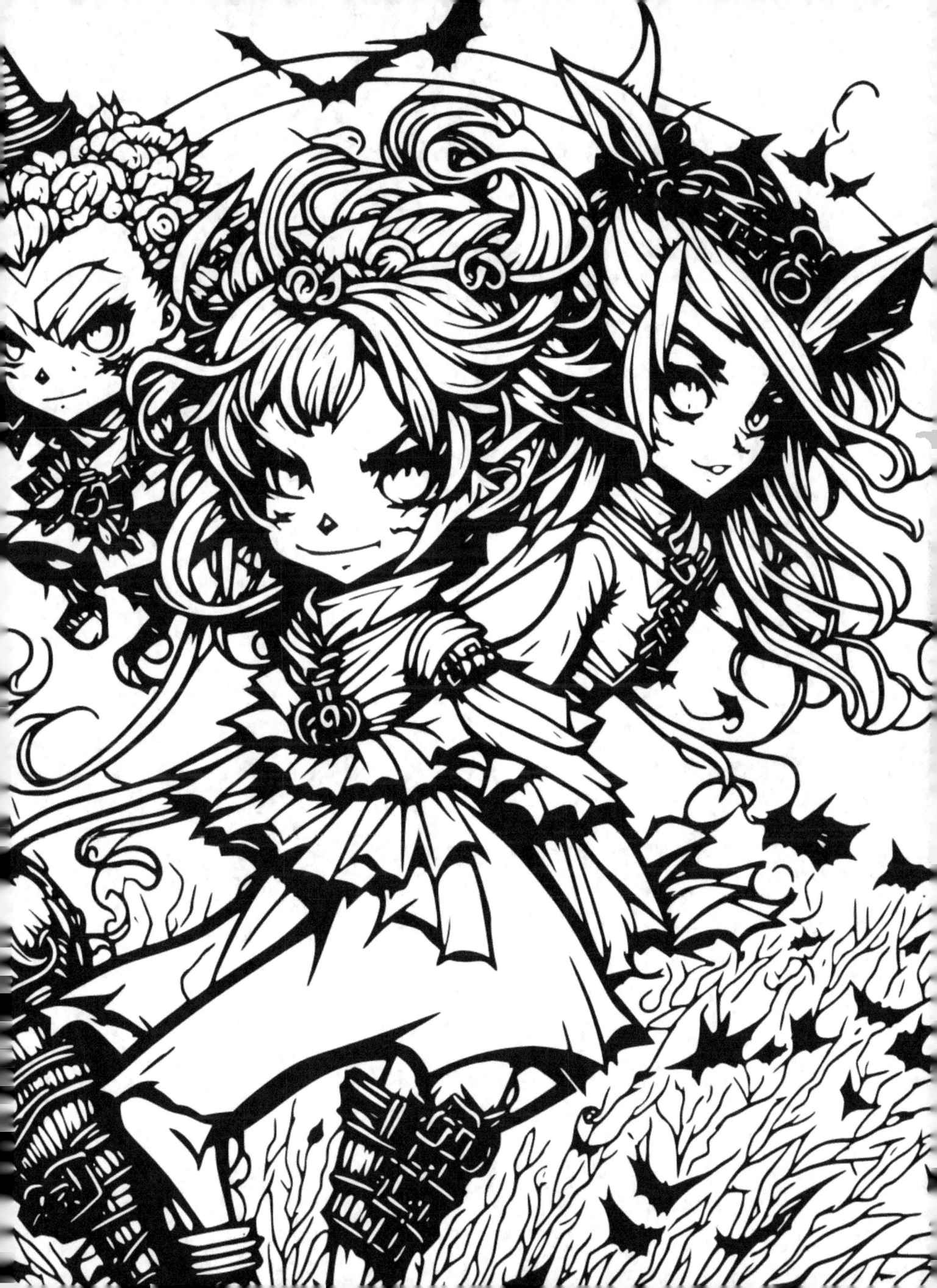

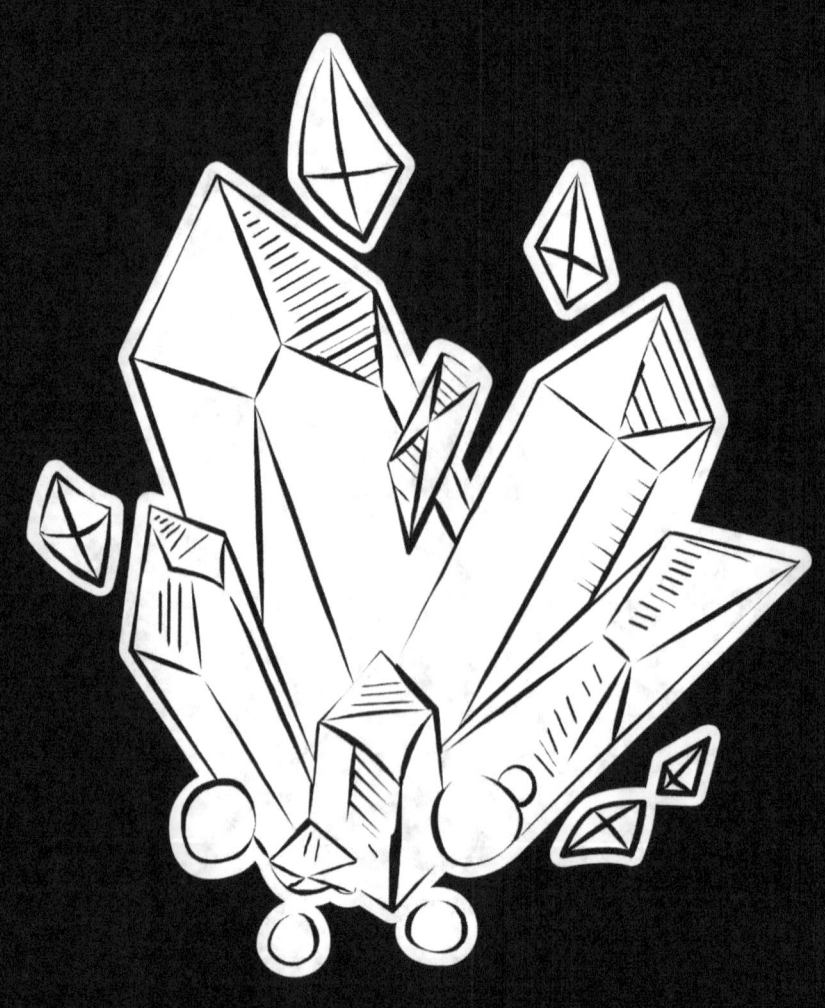

WARLOCKPUBLISHING.COM

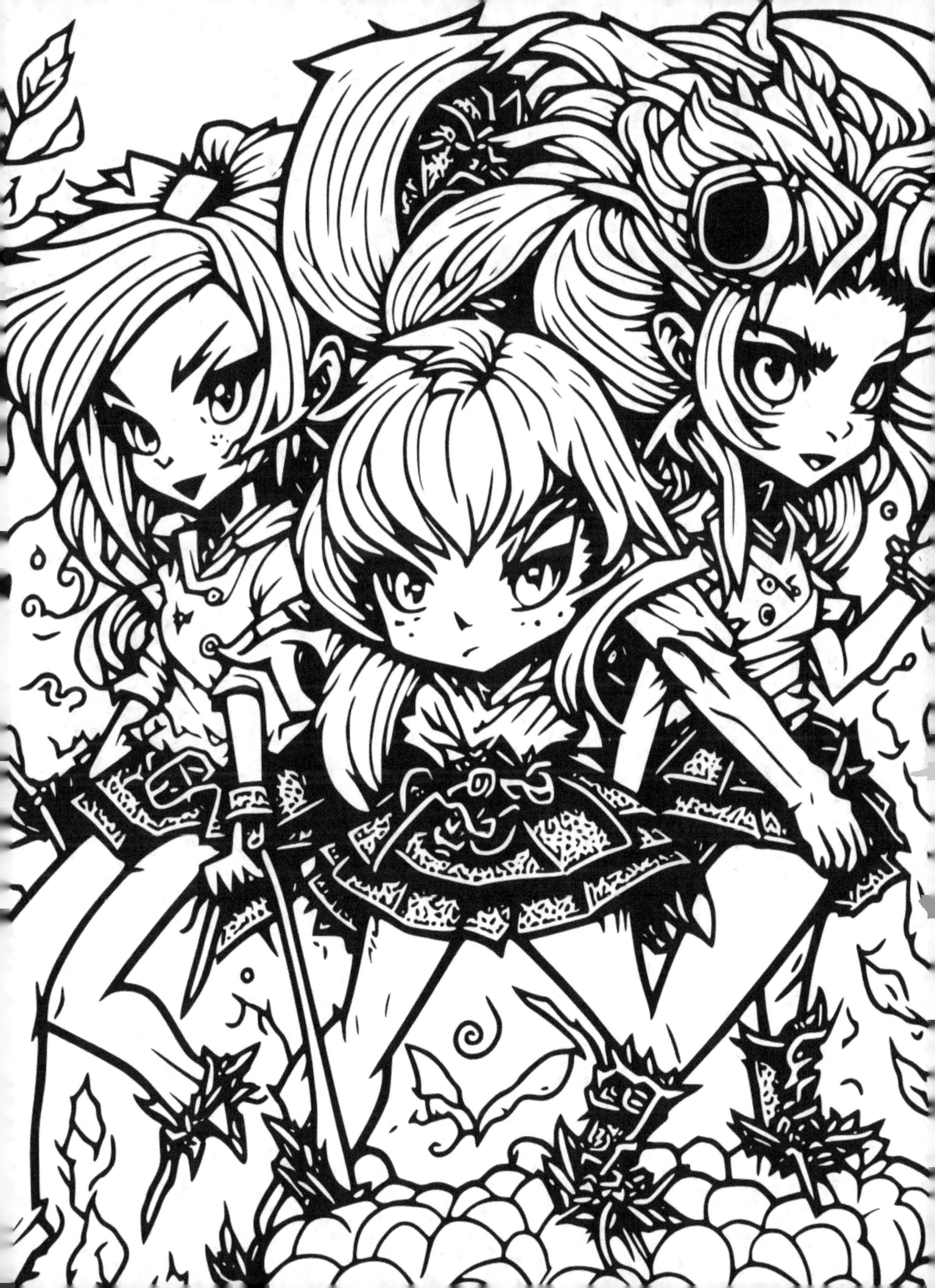

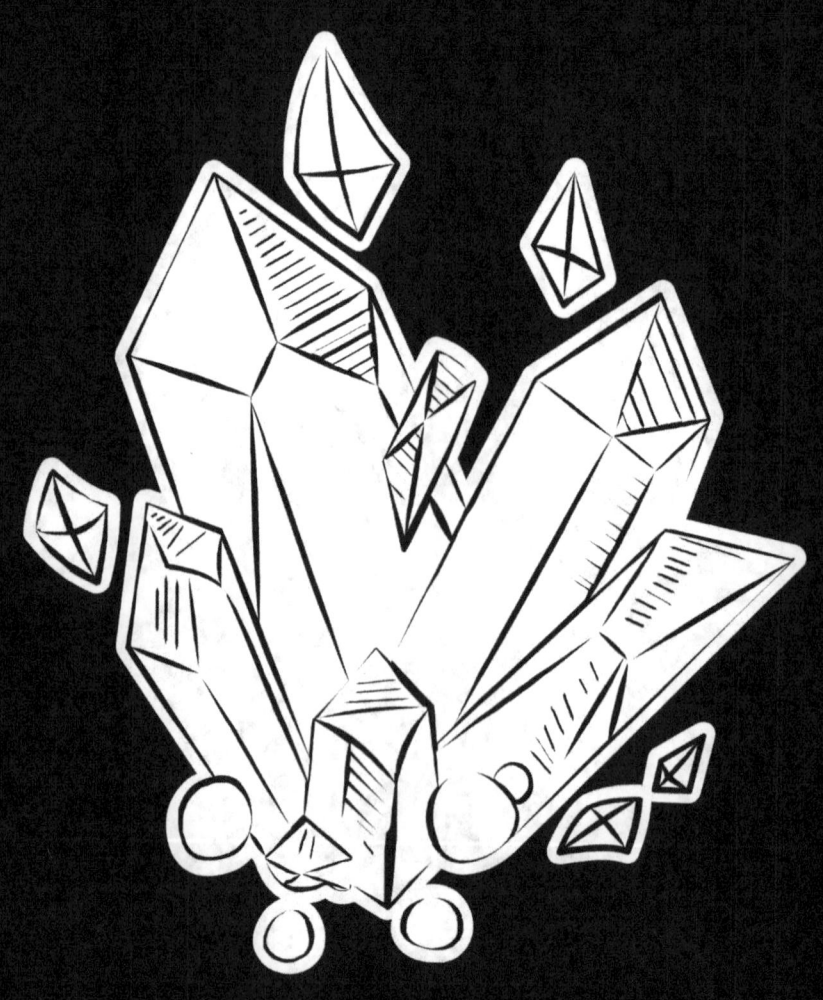

WARLOCKPUBLISHING.COM

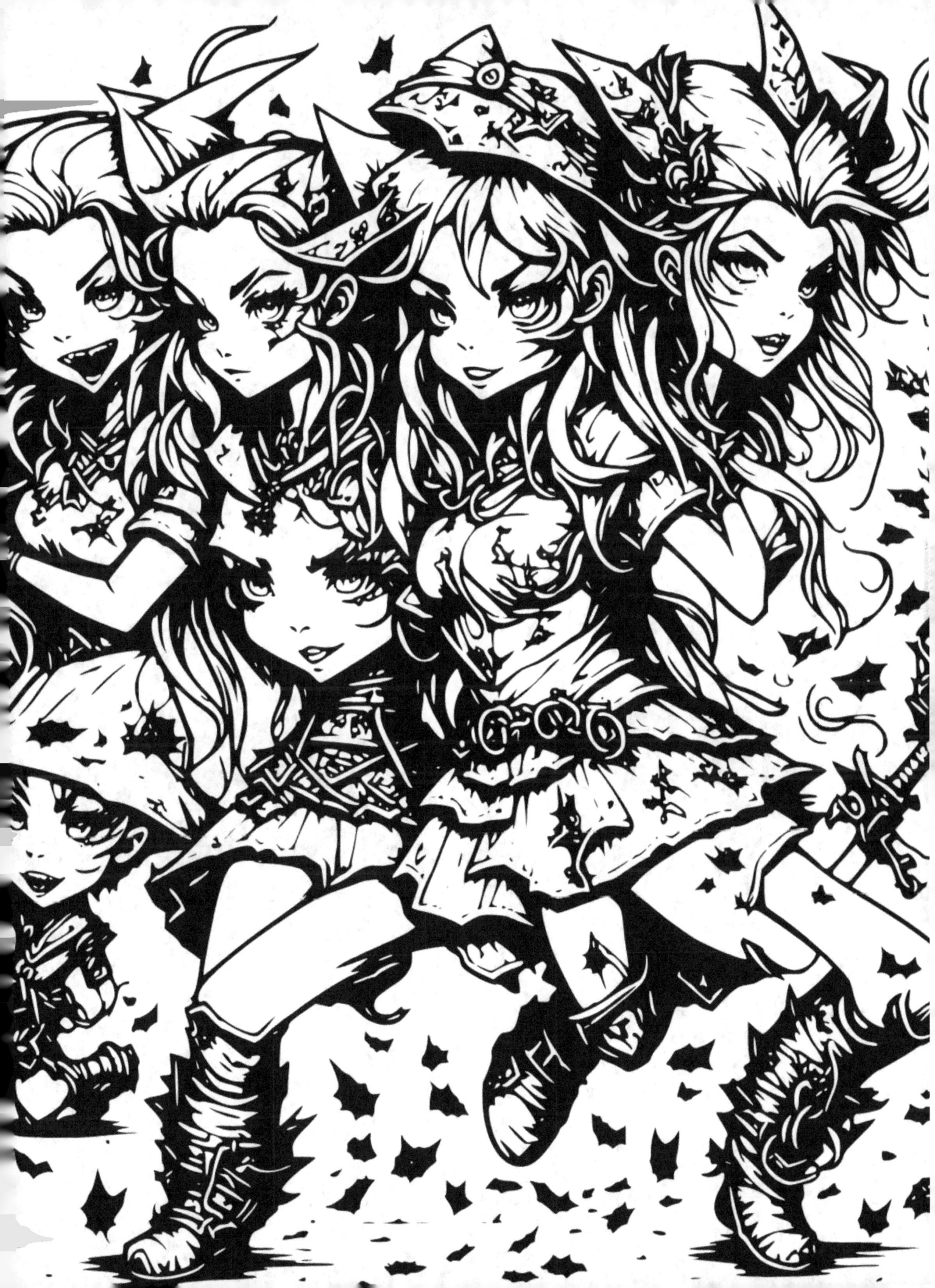

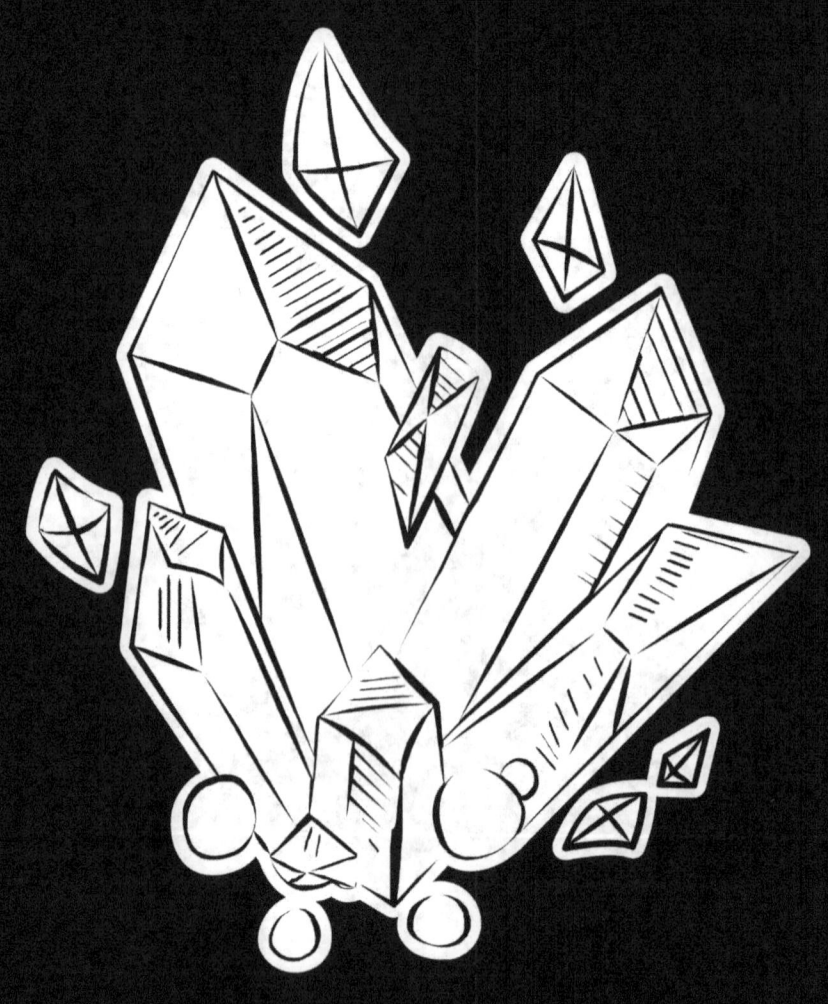

WARLOCKPUBLISHING.COM

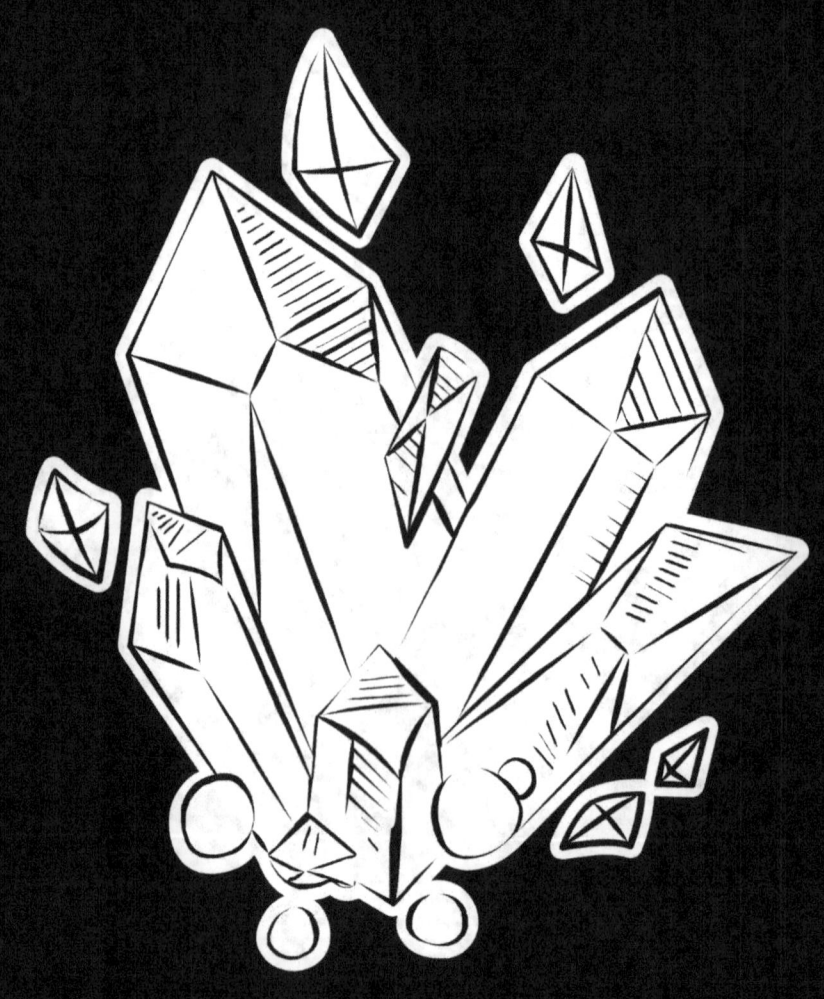

WARLOCKPUBLISHING.COM

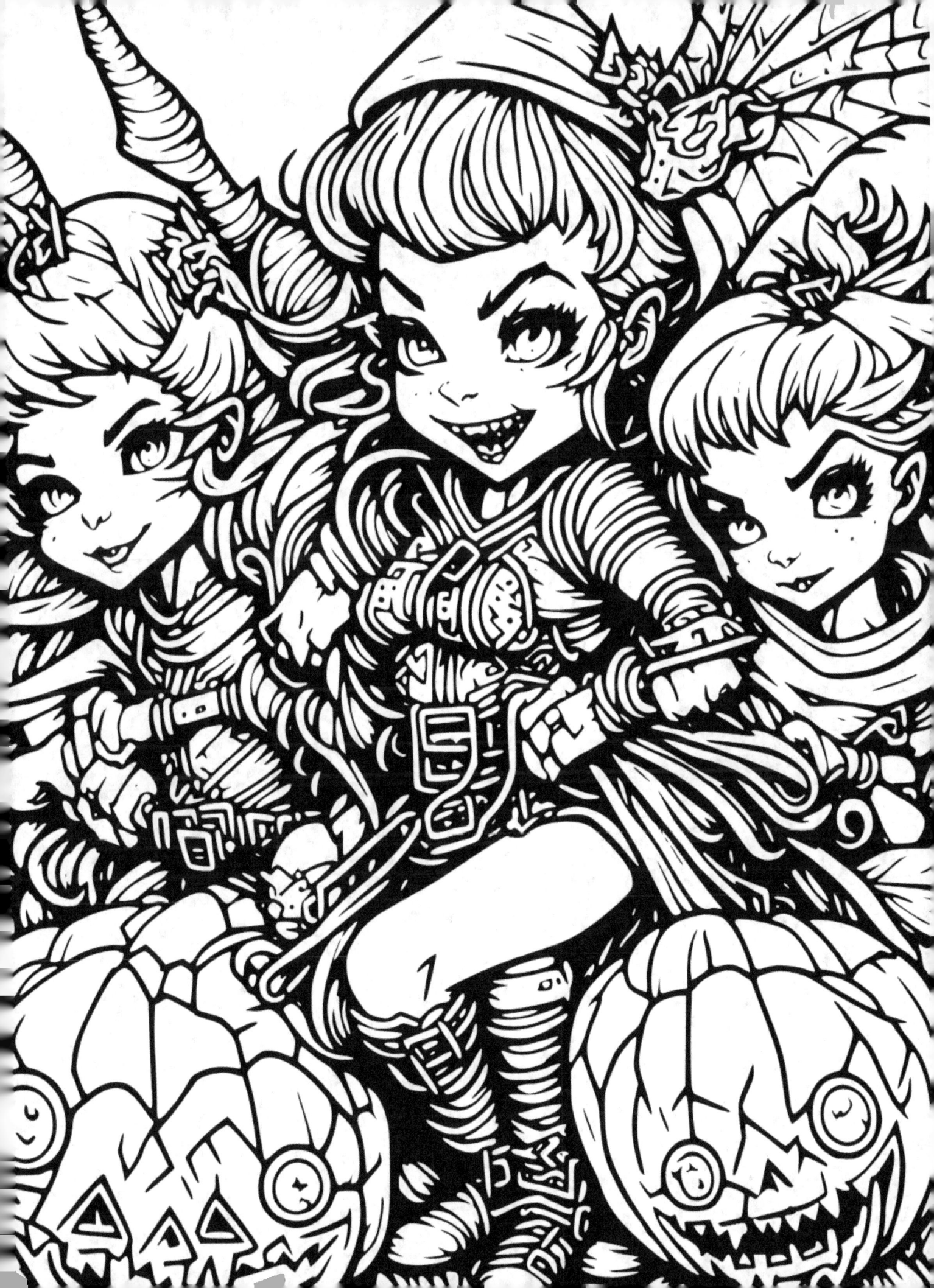

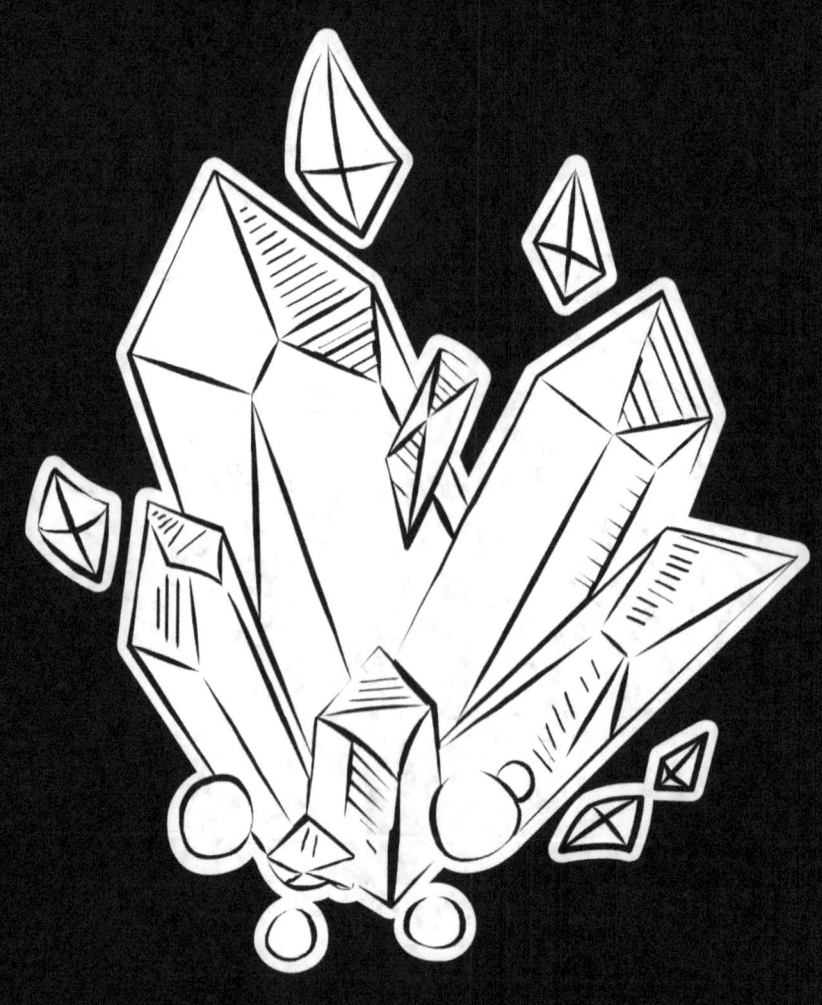

WARLOCKPUBLISHING.COM

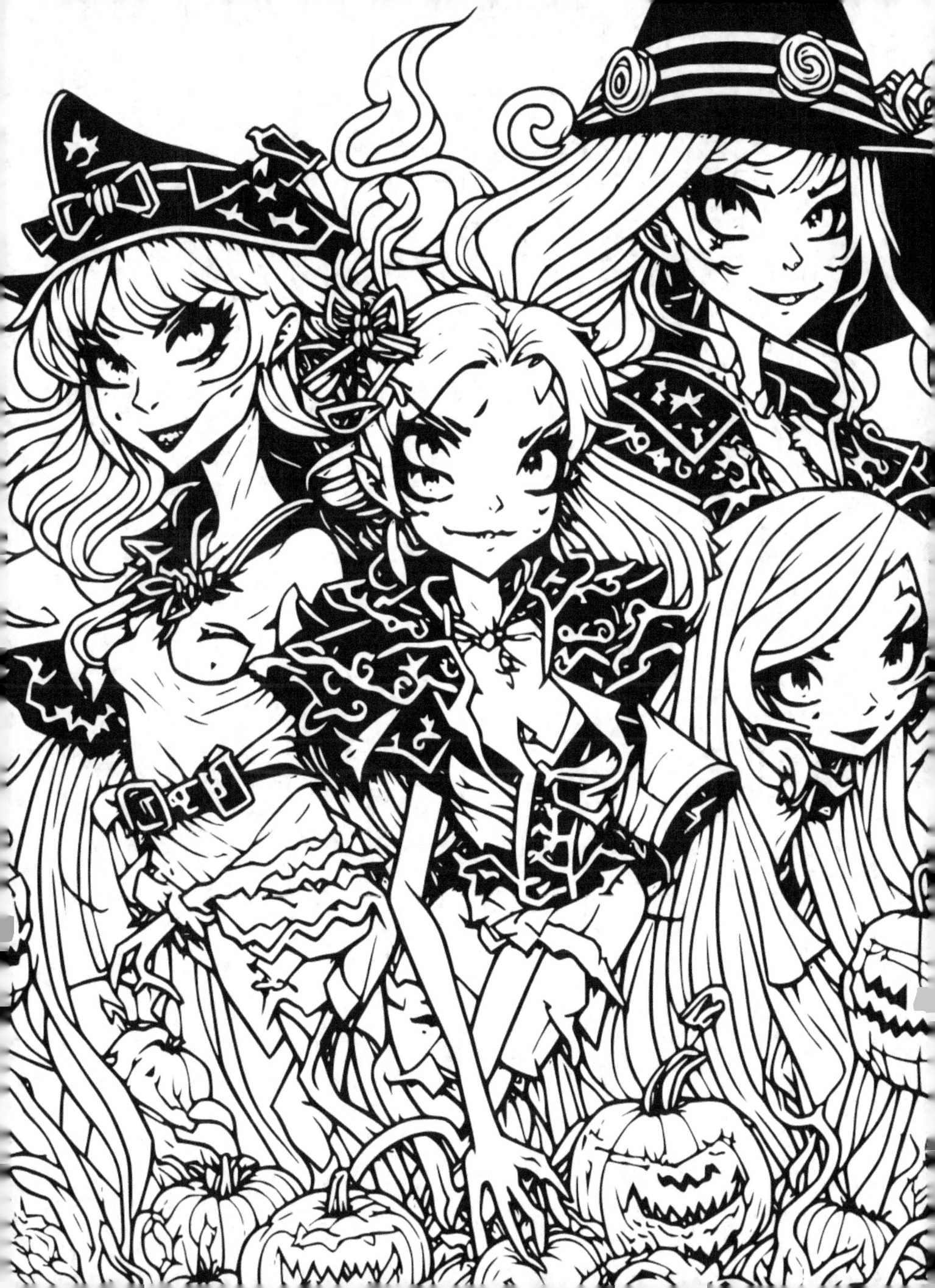

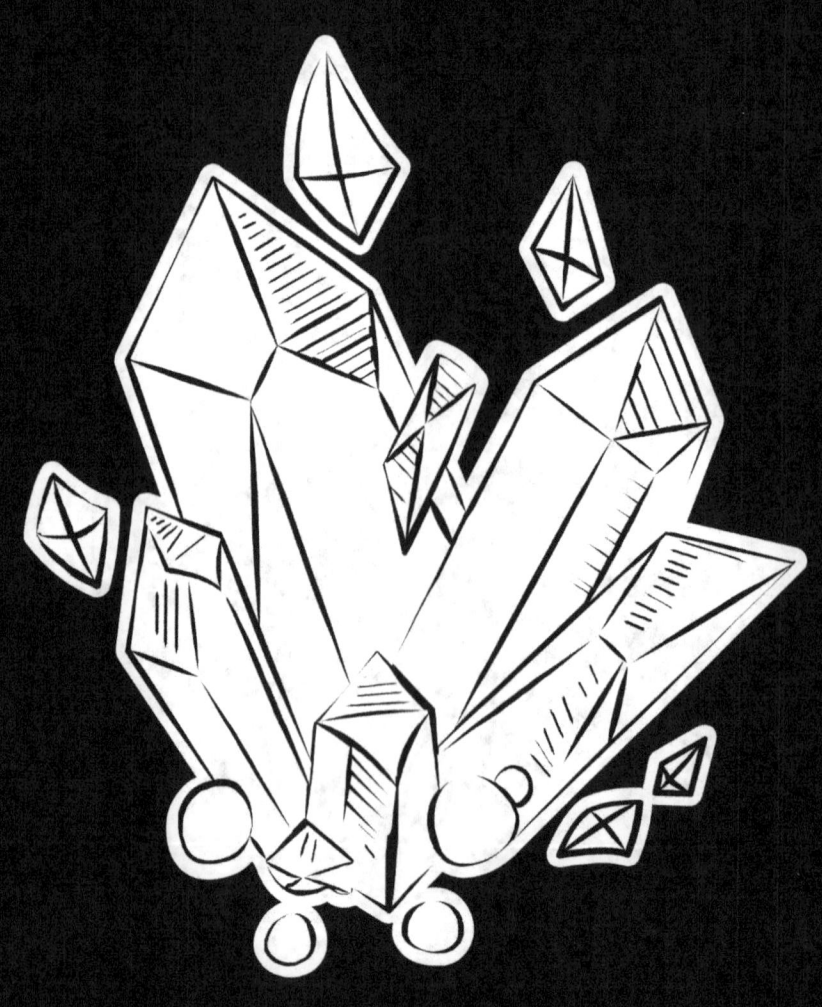

WARLOCKPUBLISHING.COM

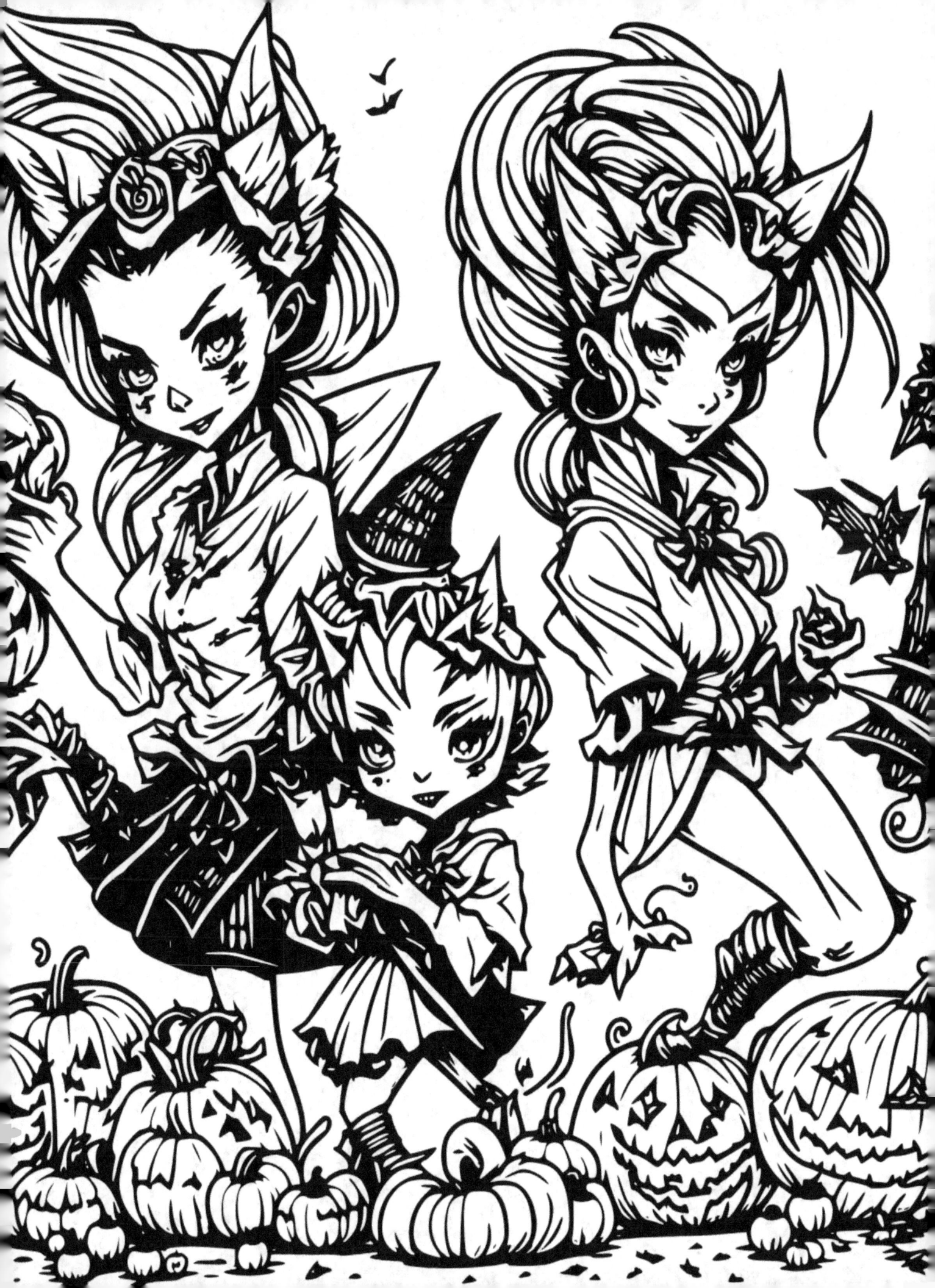

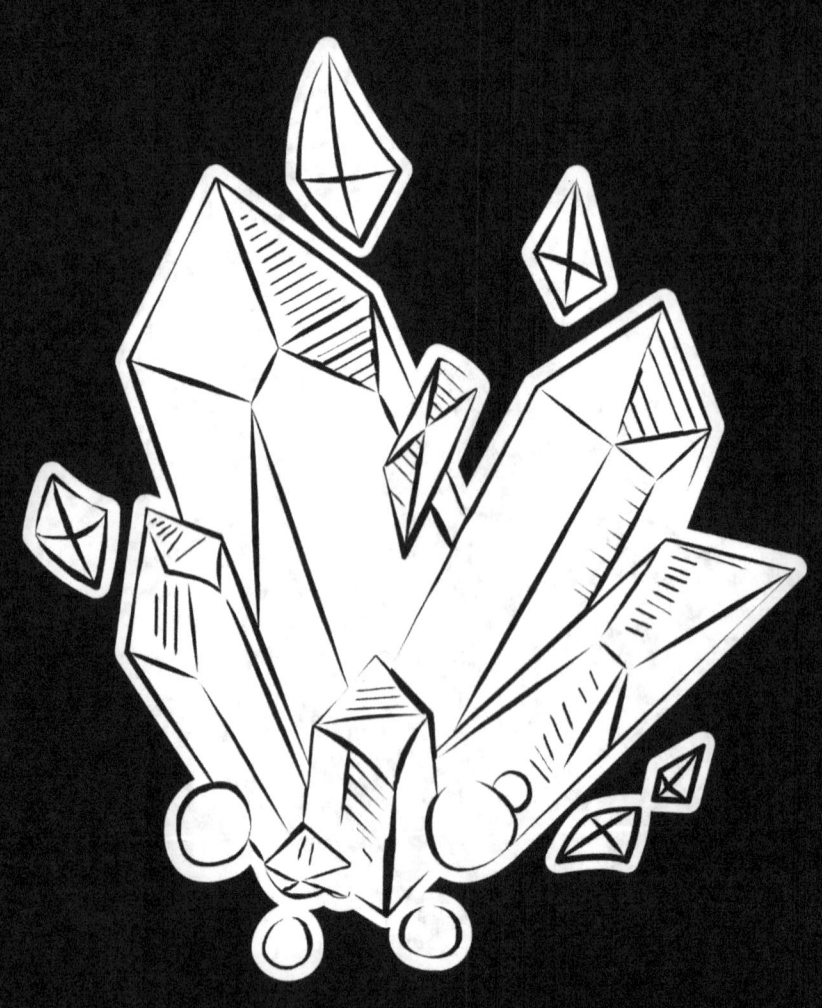

WARLOCKPUBLISHING.COM

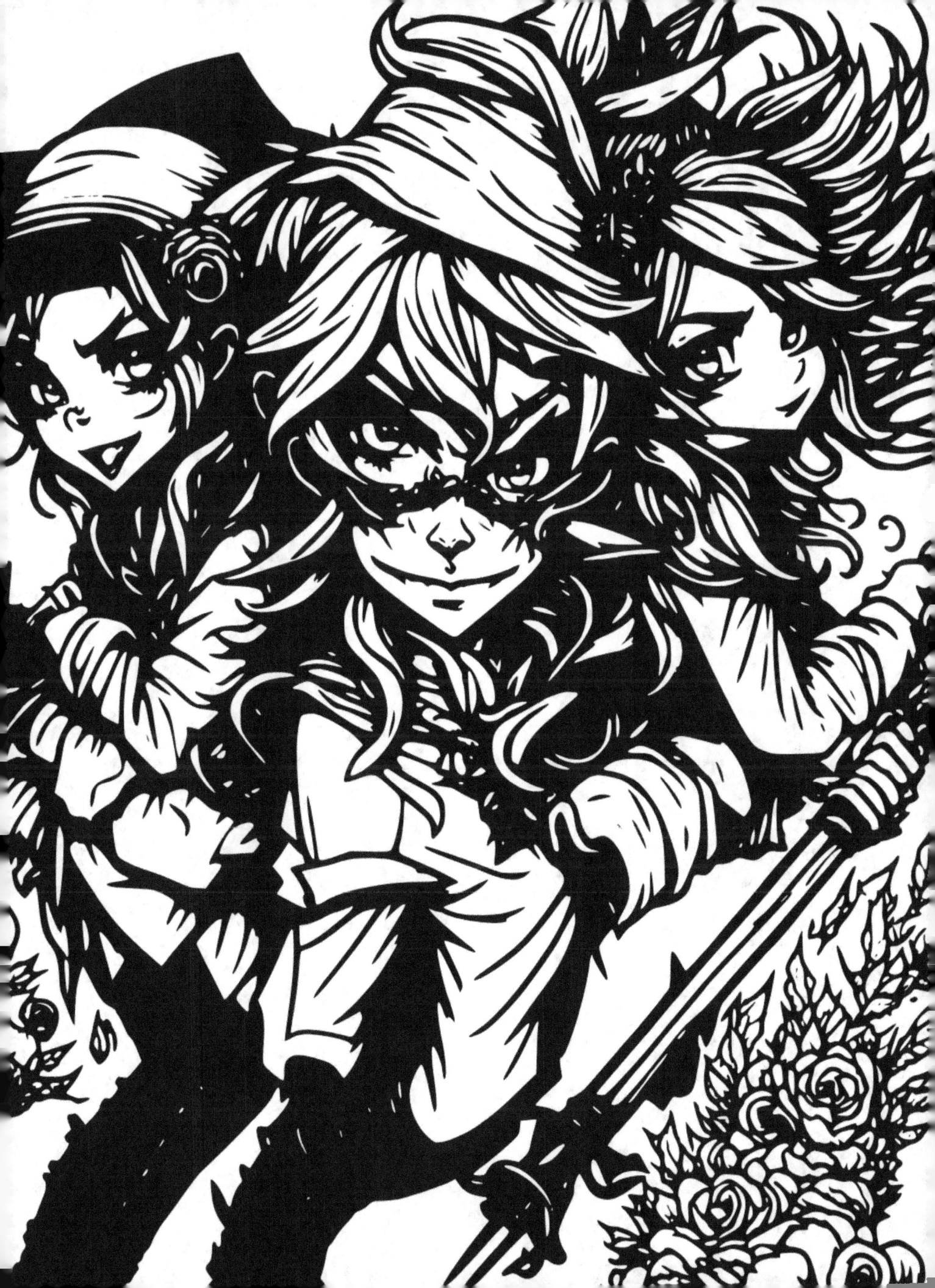

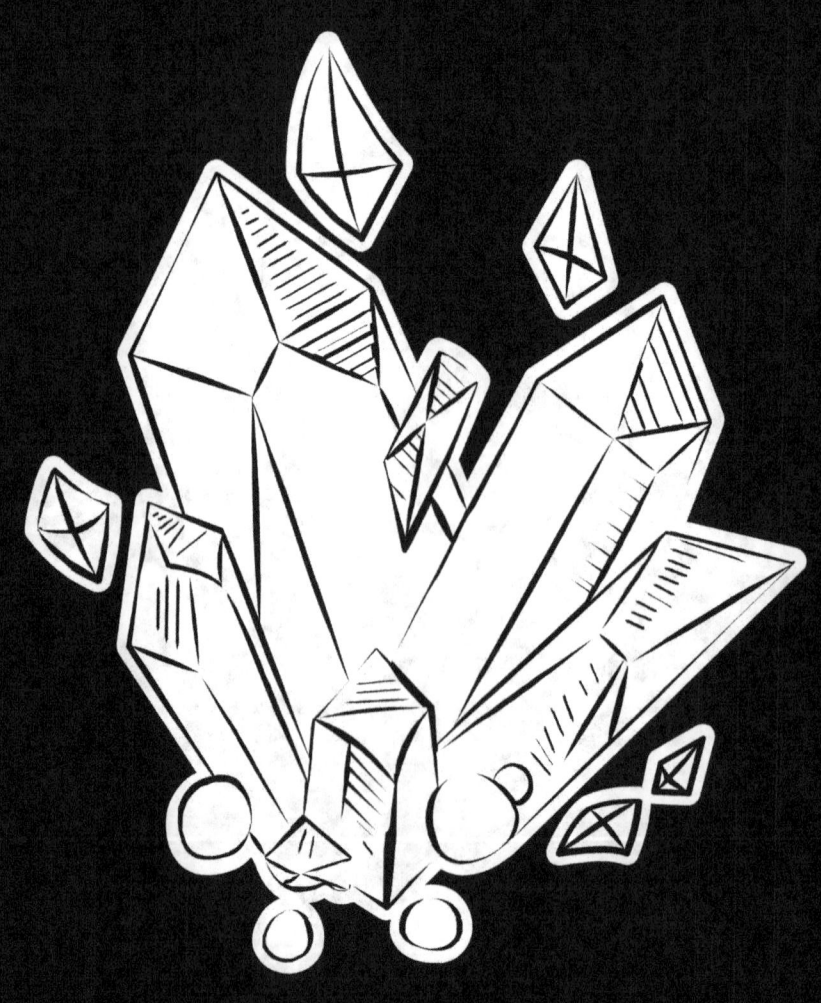

WARLOCKPUBLISHING.COM

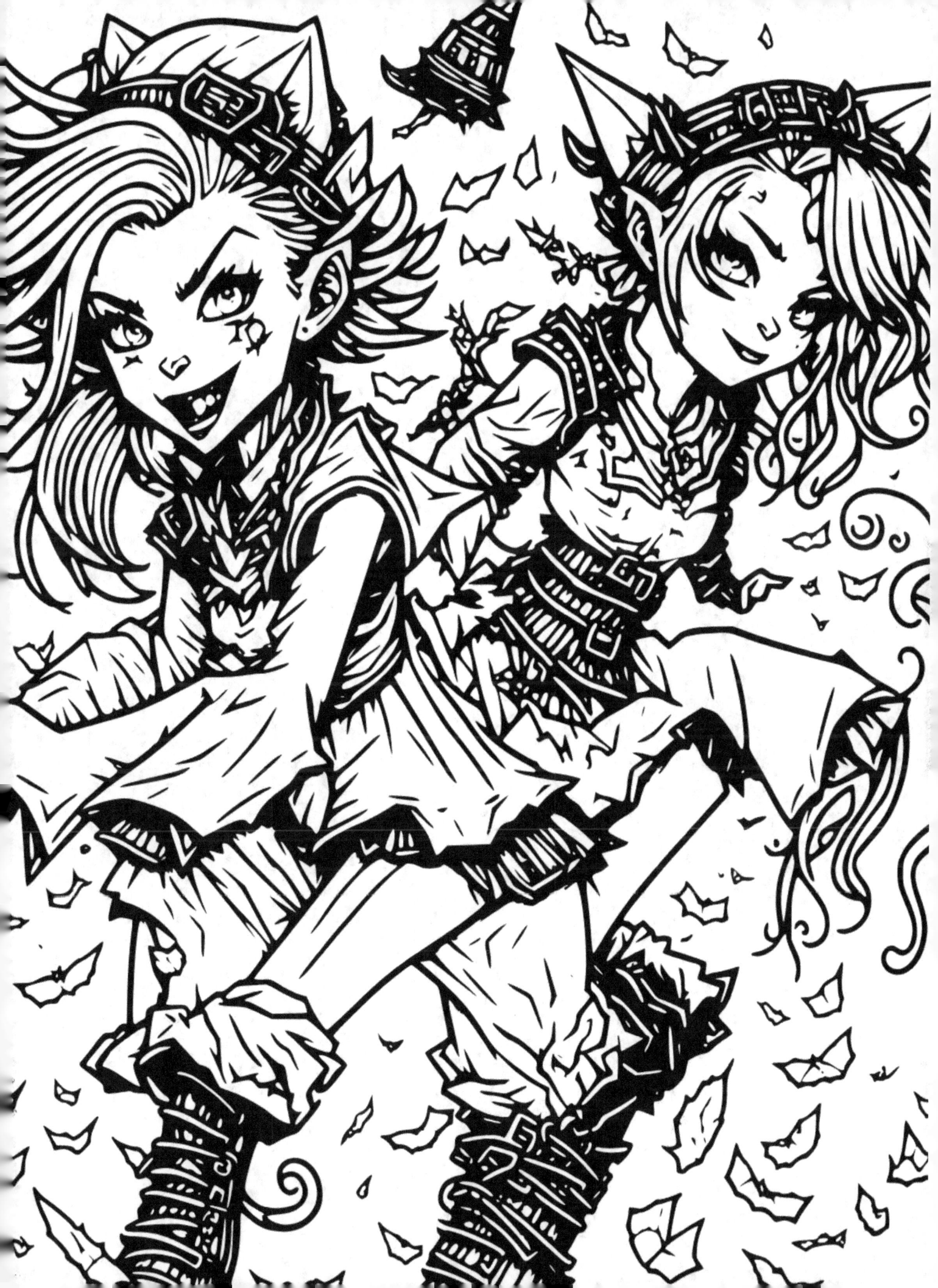

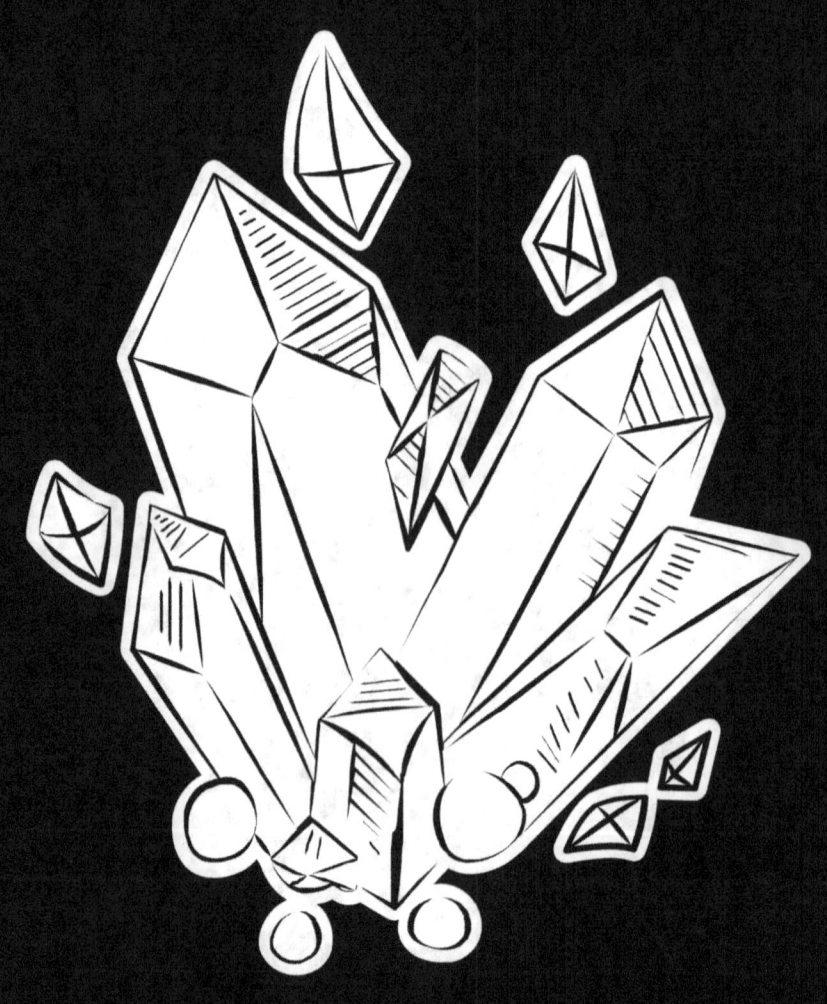

WARLOCKPUBLISHING.COM

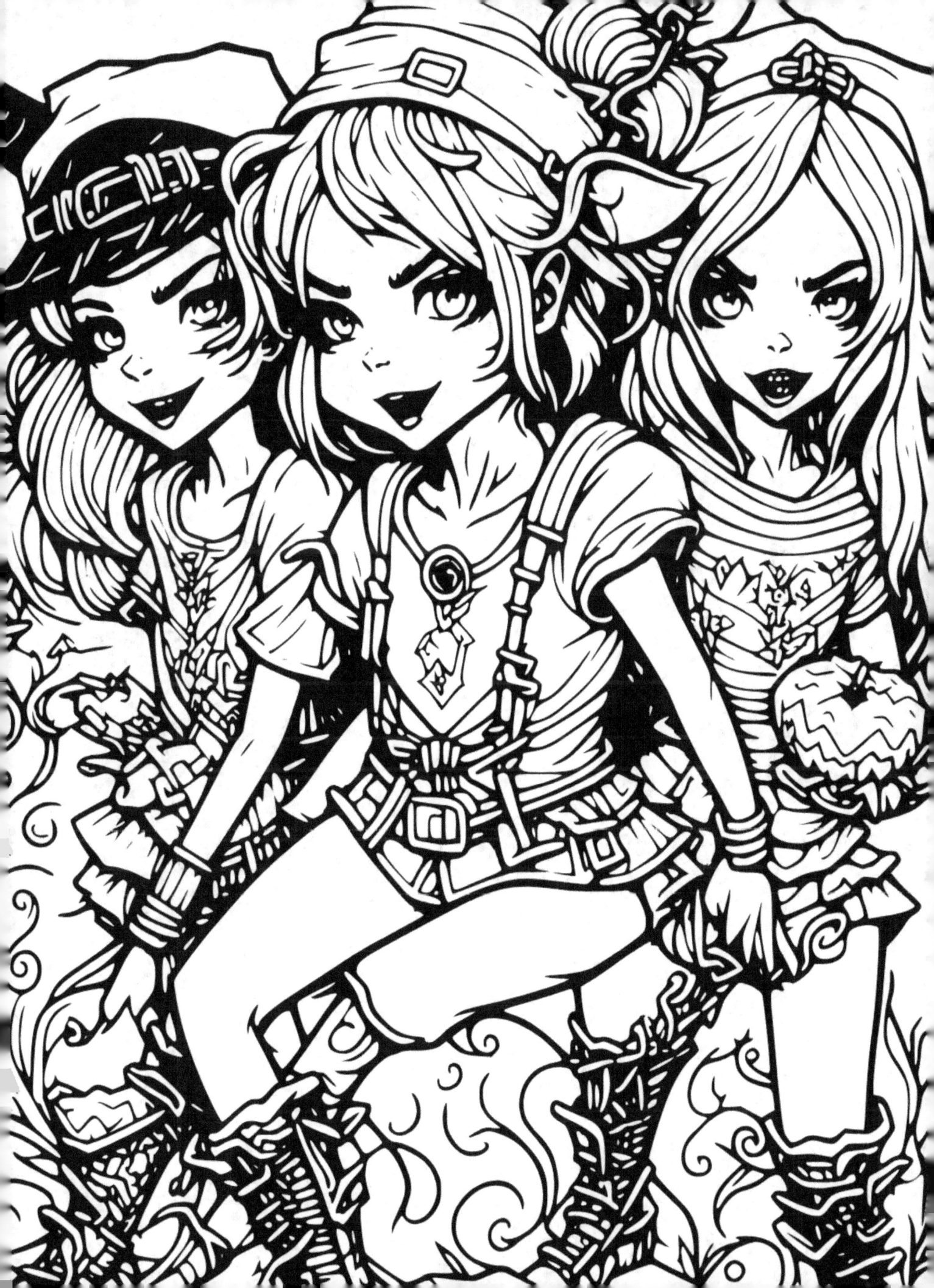

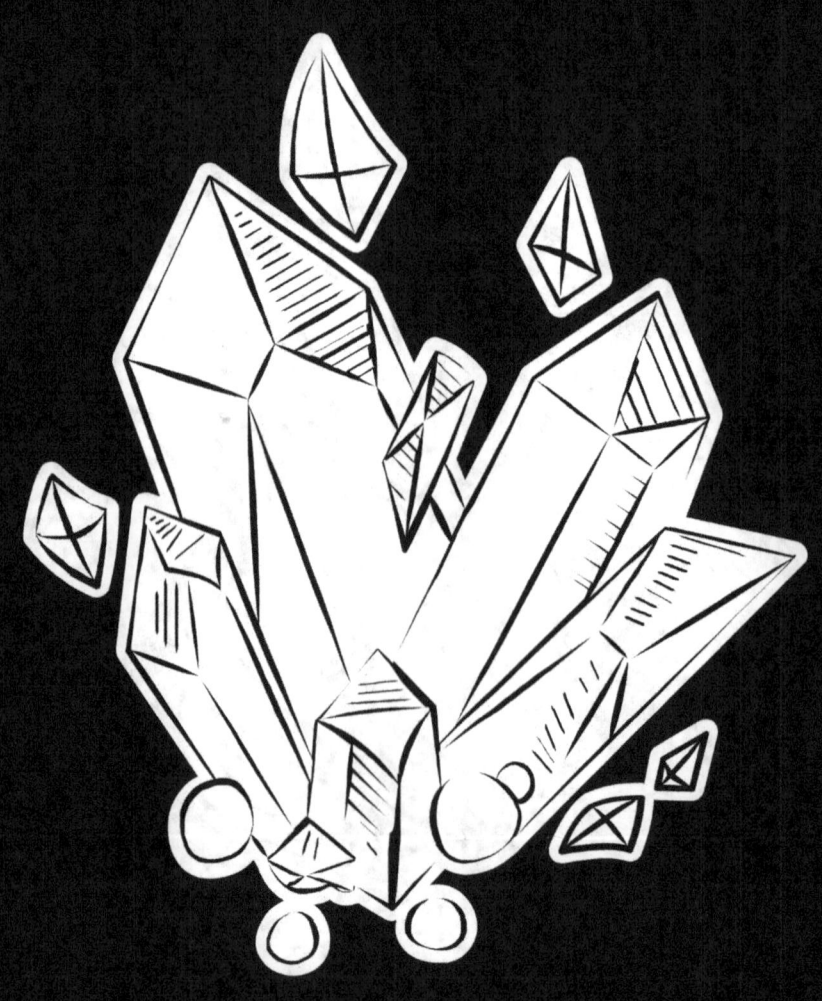

WARLOCKPUBLISHING.COM

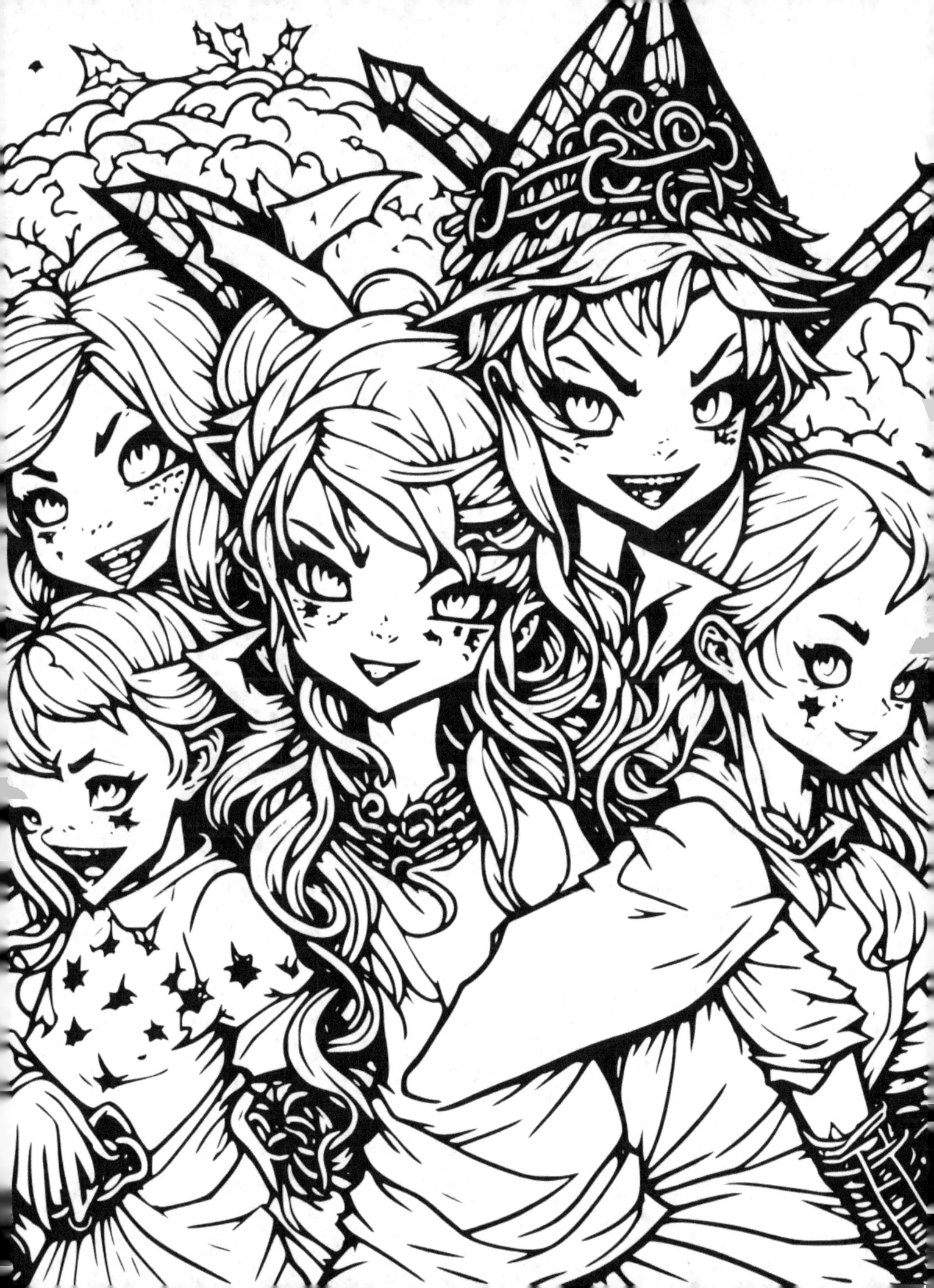

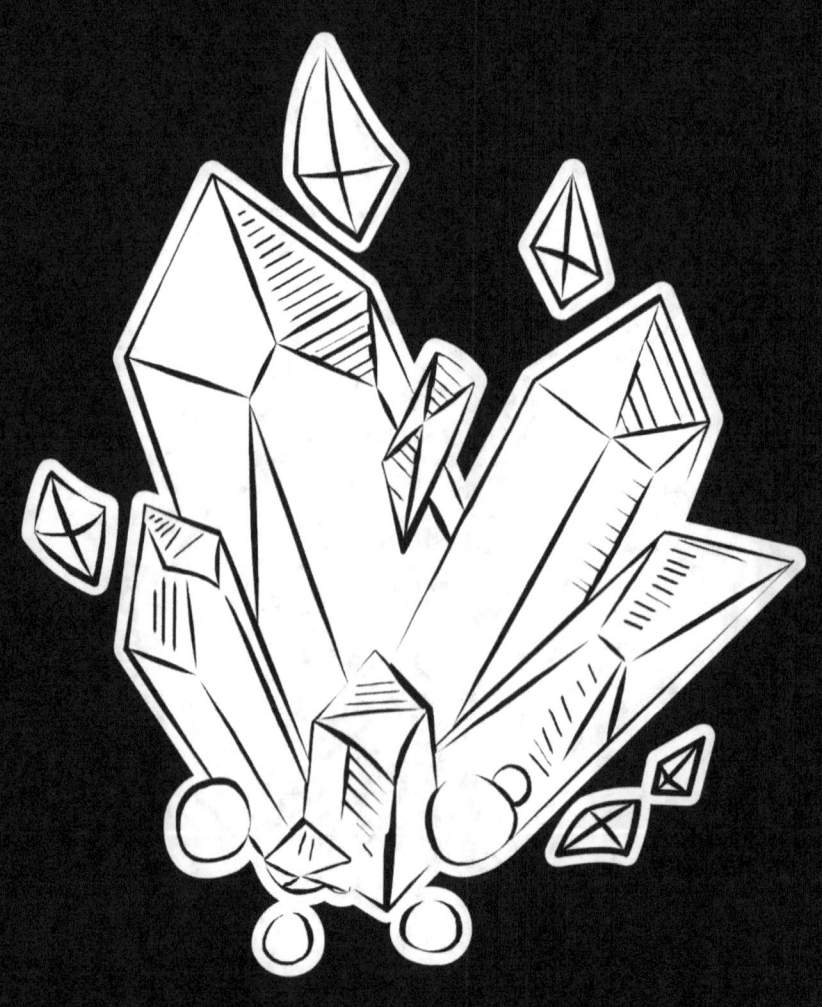

WARLOCKPUBLISHING.COM

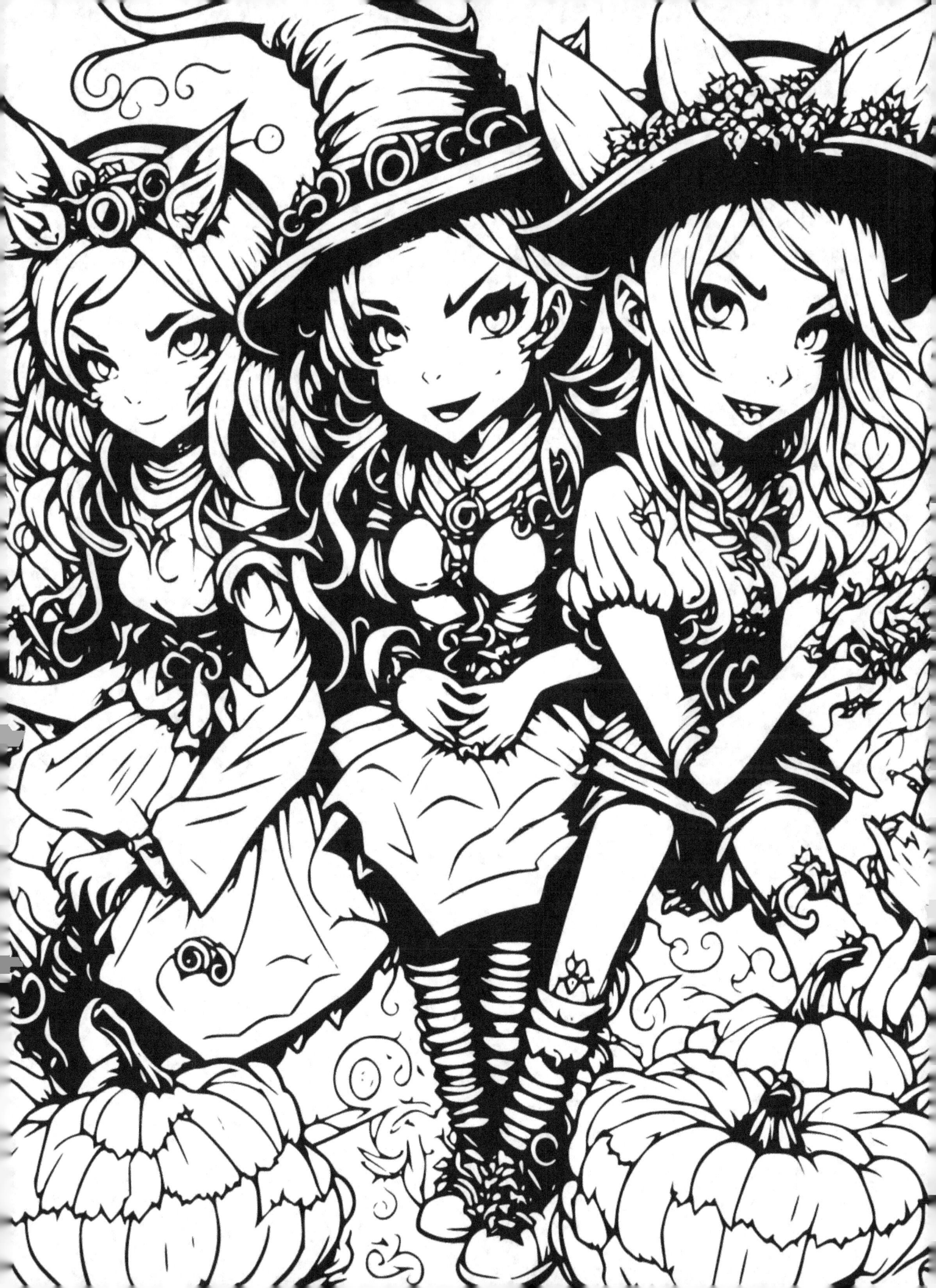

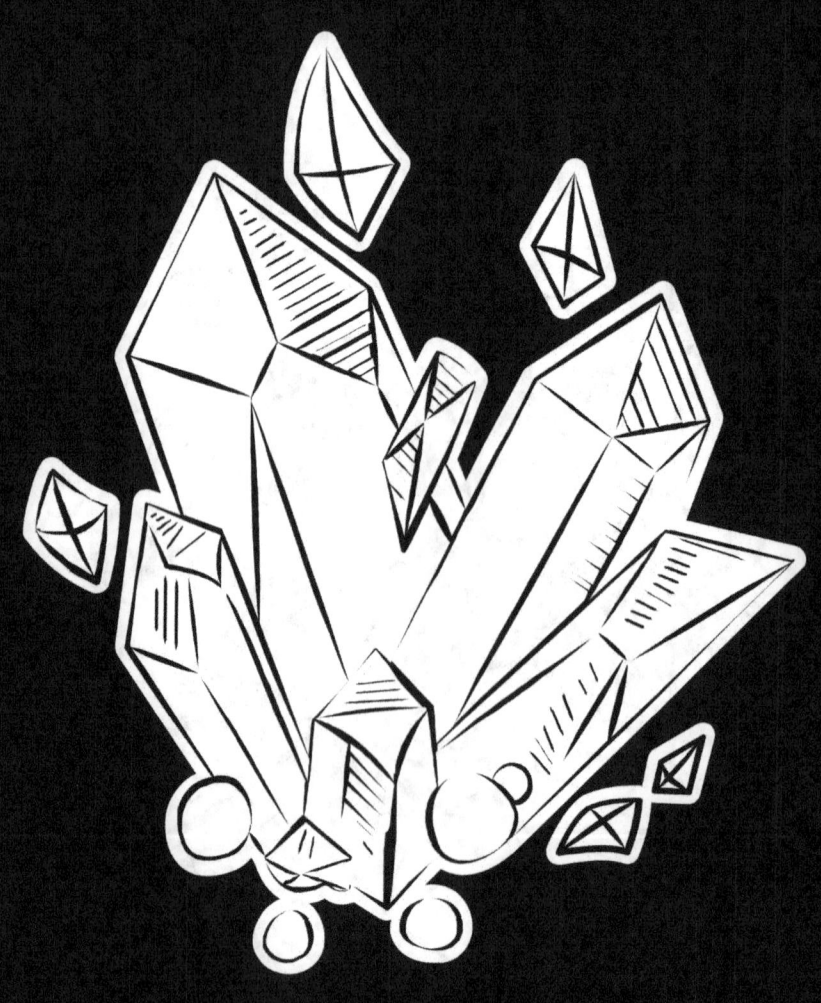

WARLOCKPUBLISHING.COM

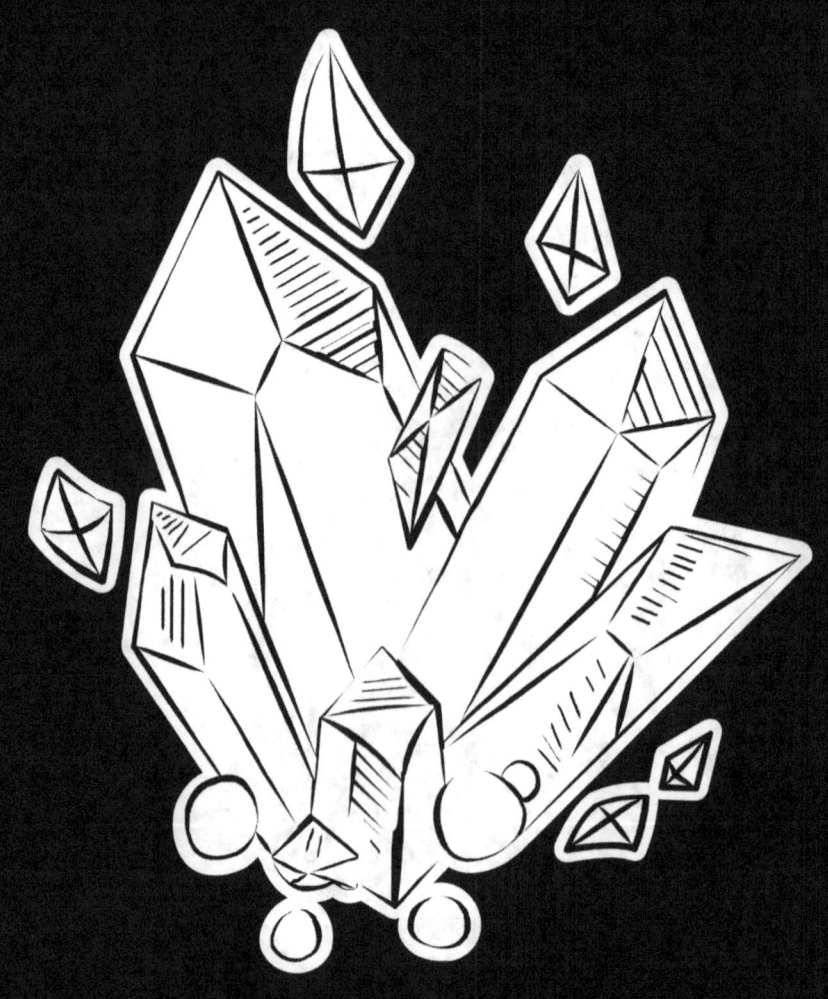

WARLOCKPUBLISHINE.COM

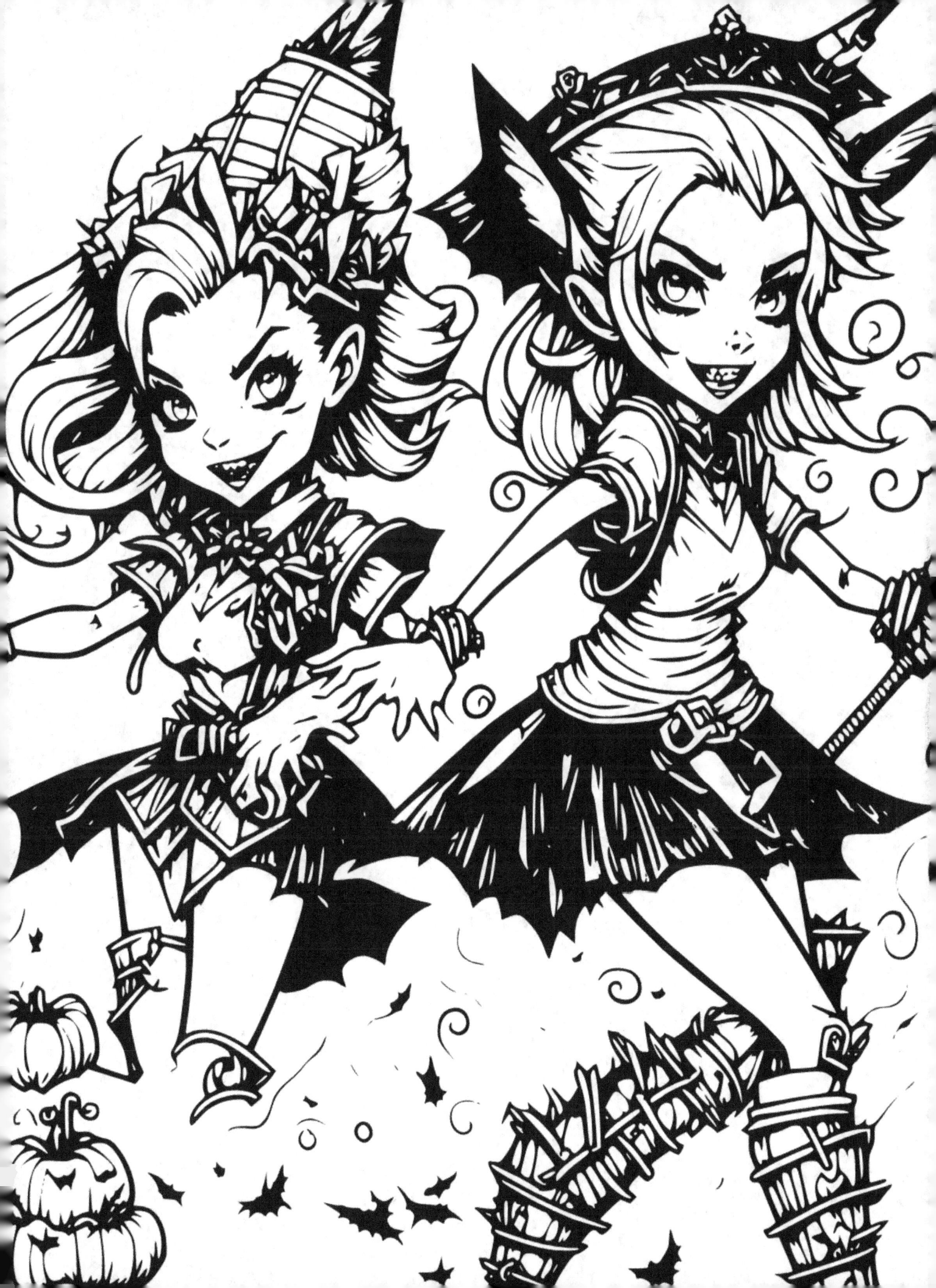

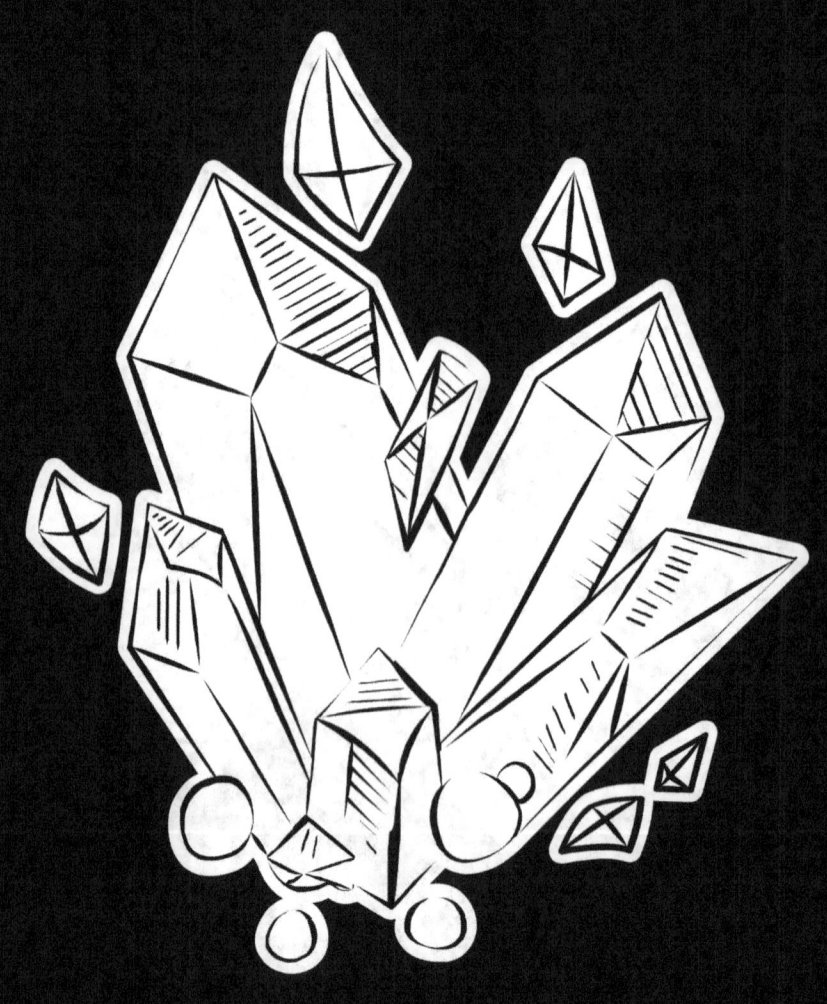

WARLOCKPUBLISHING.COM

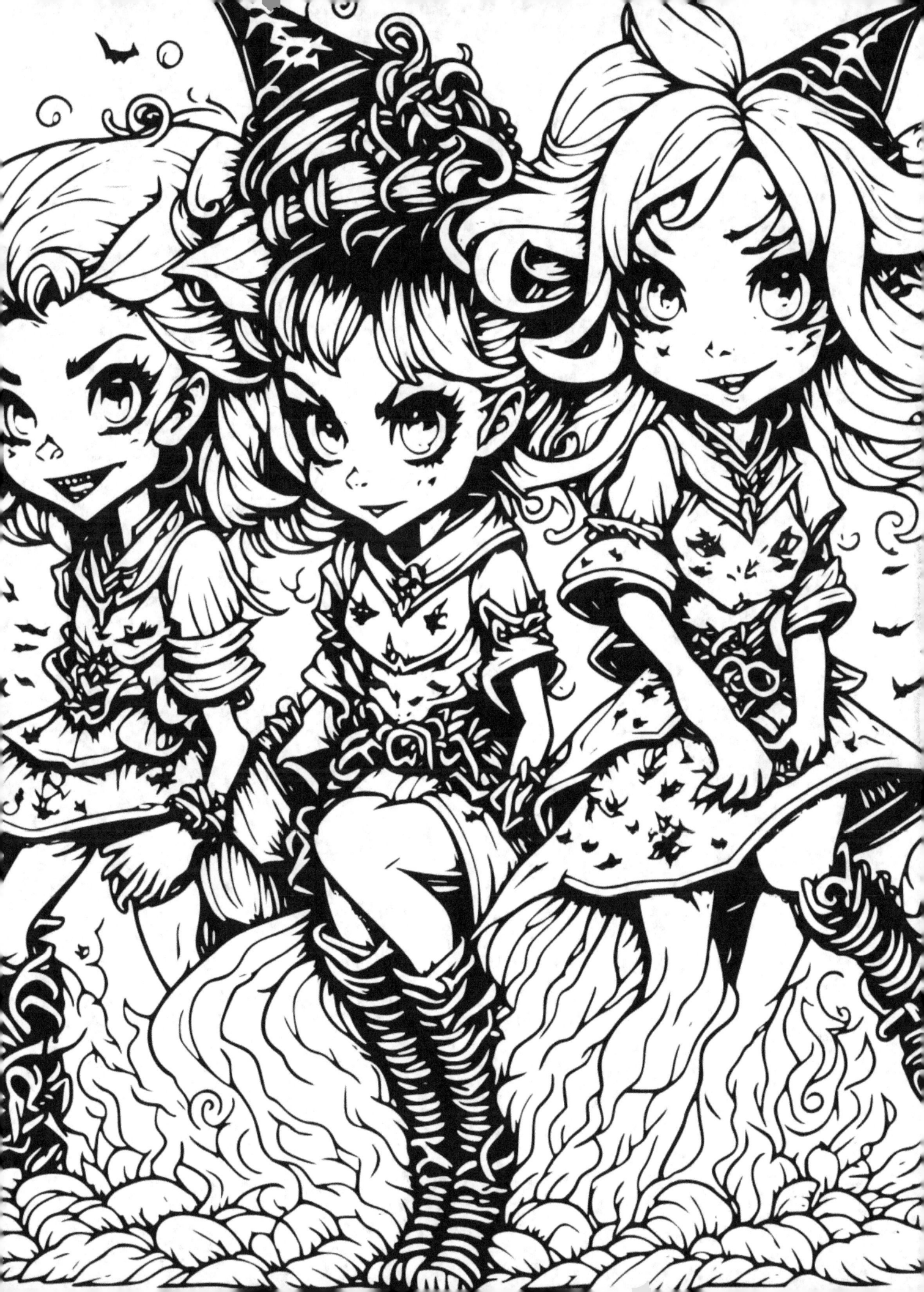

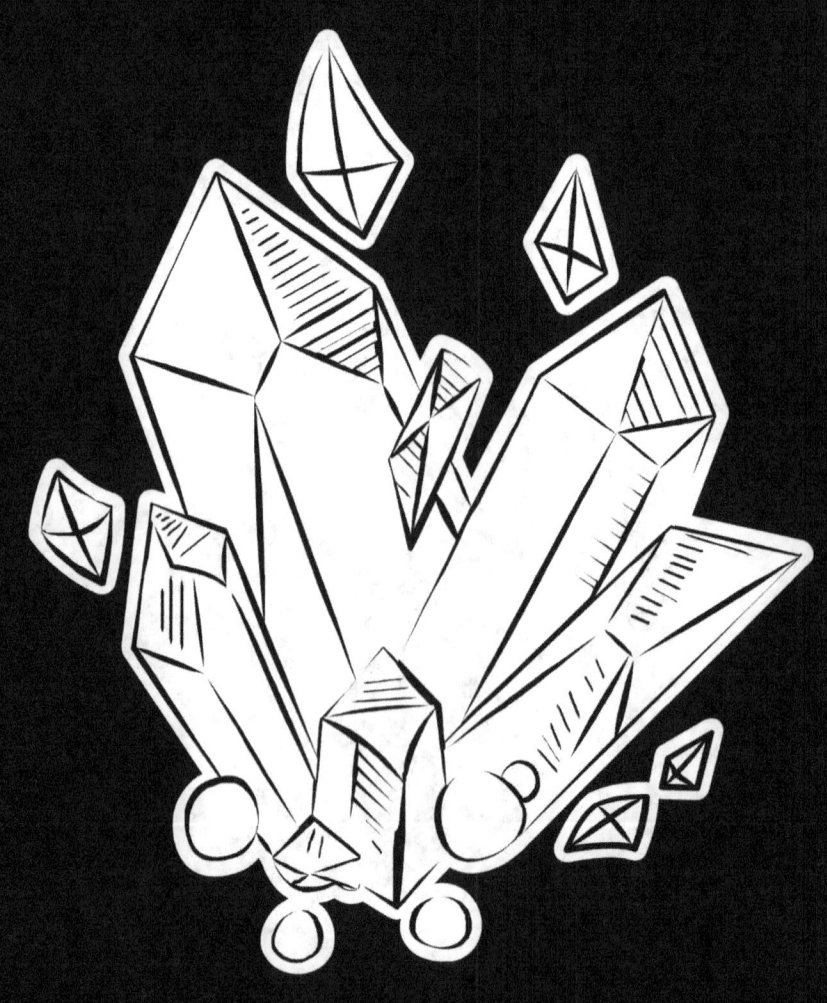

WARLOCKPUBLISHING.COM

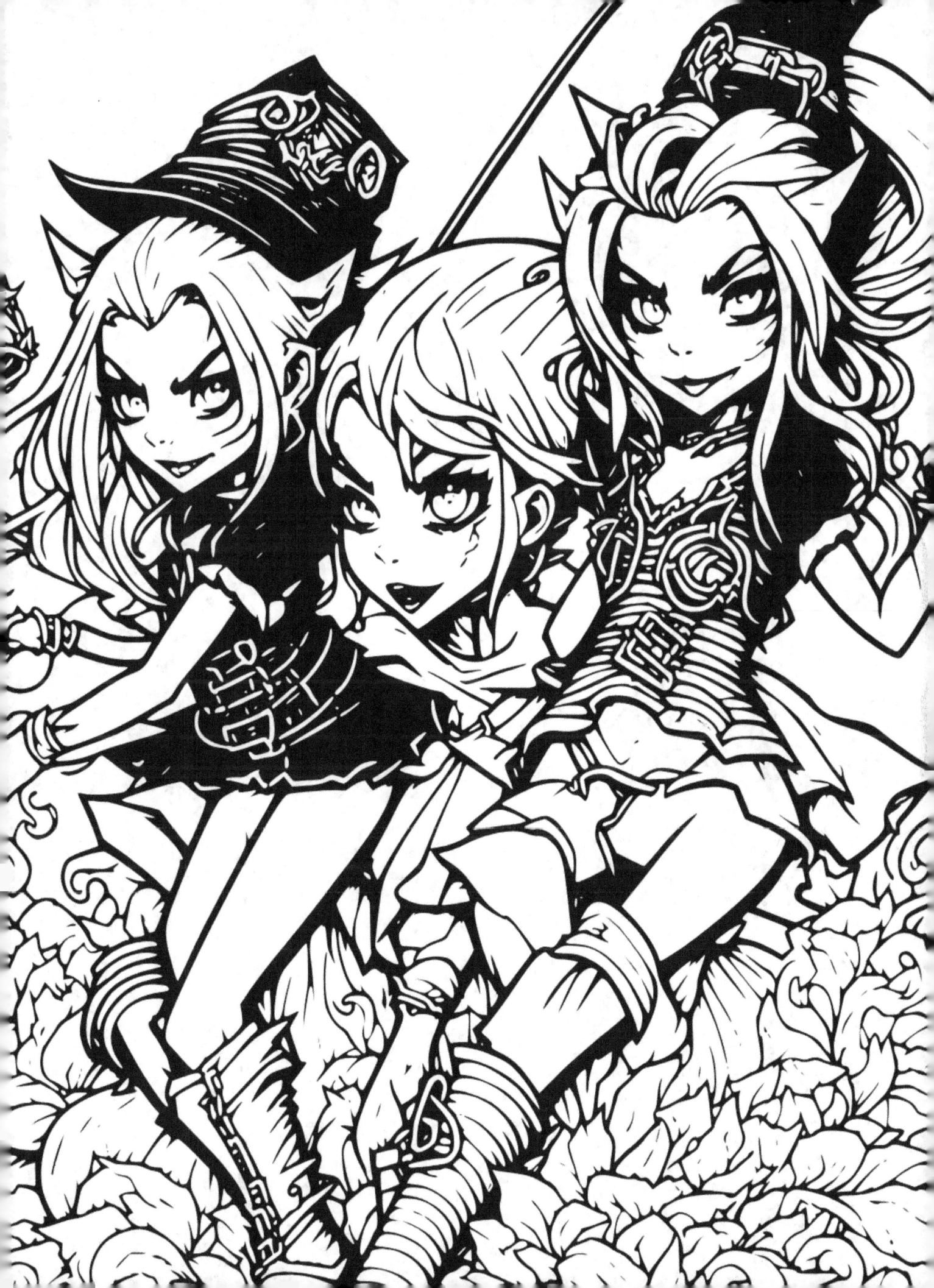

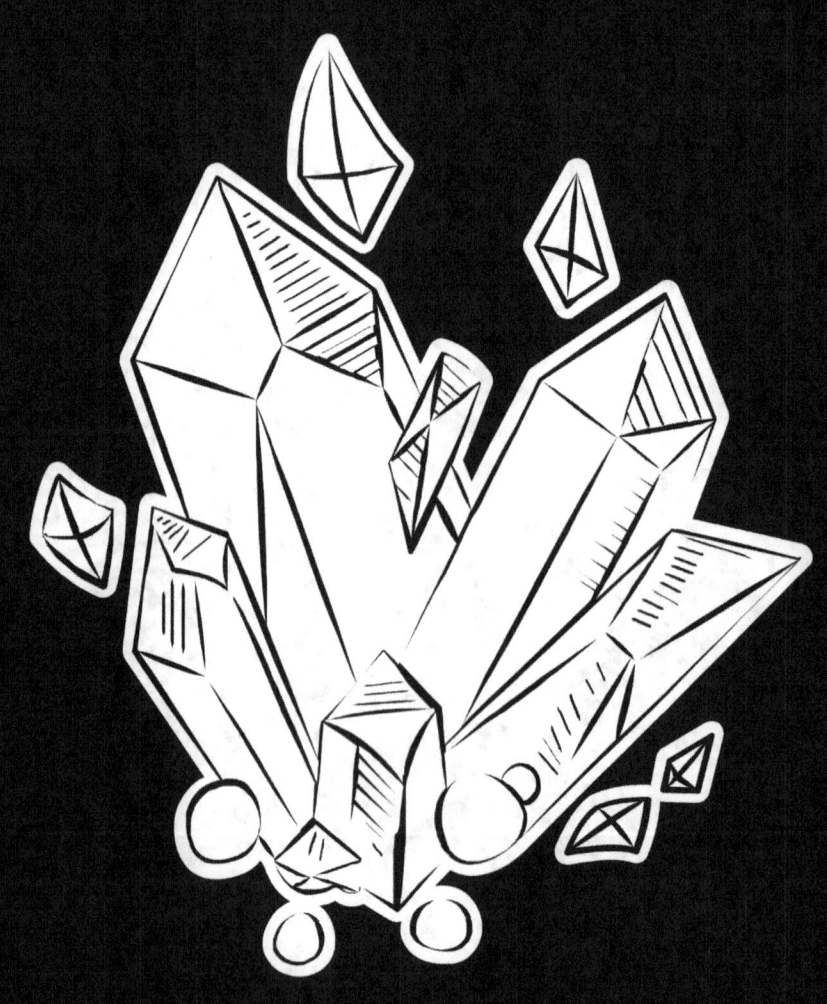

WARLOCKPUBLISHING.COM

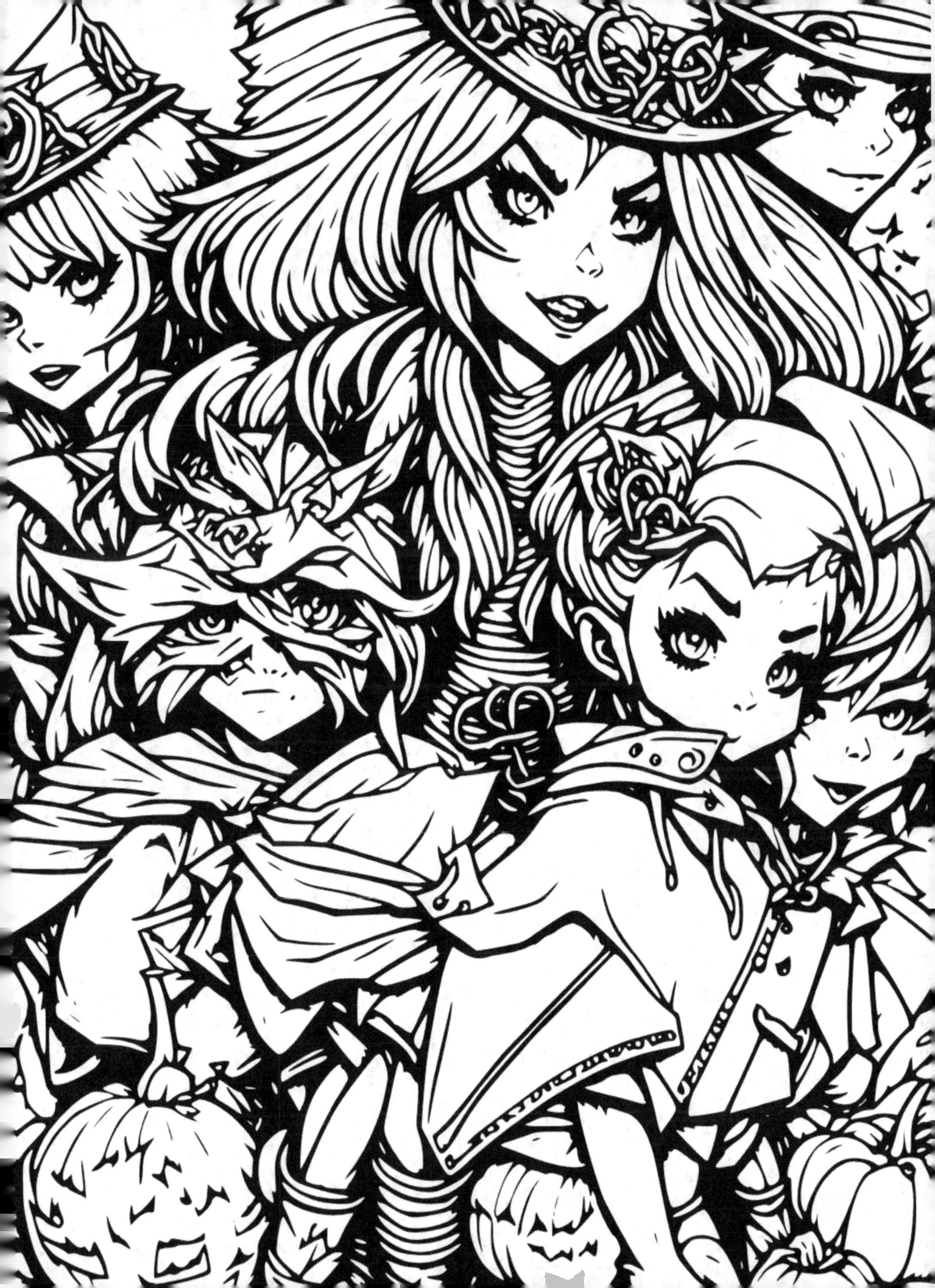

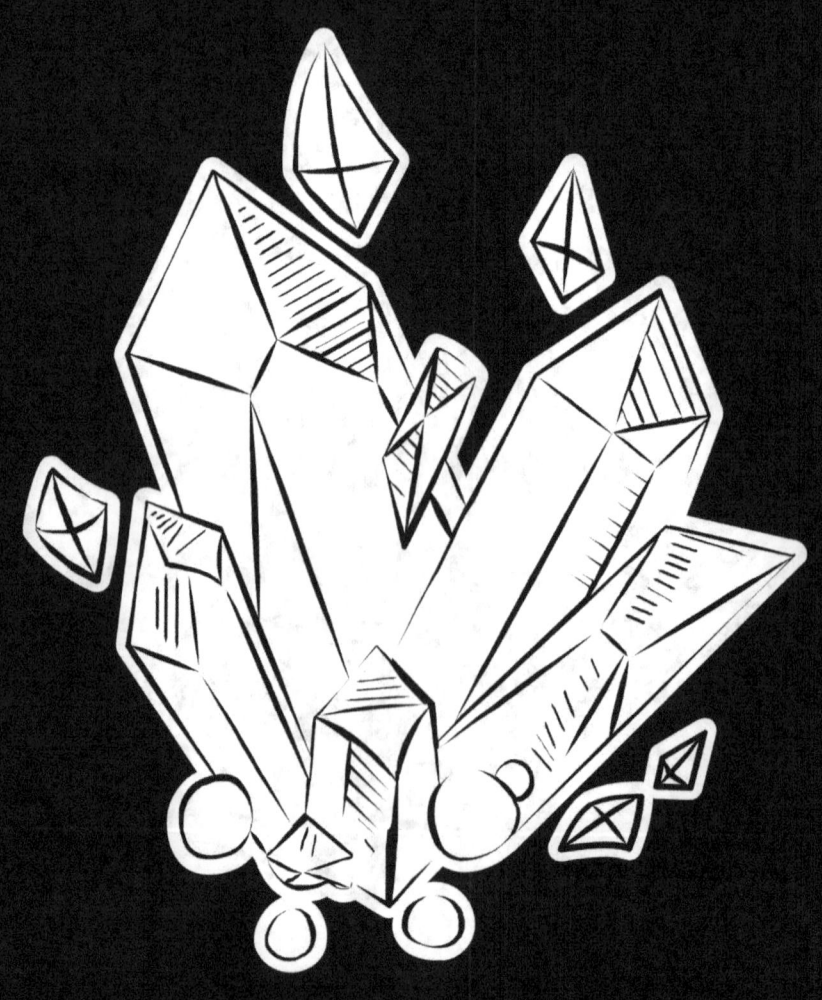

WARLOCKPUBLISHING.COM

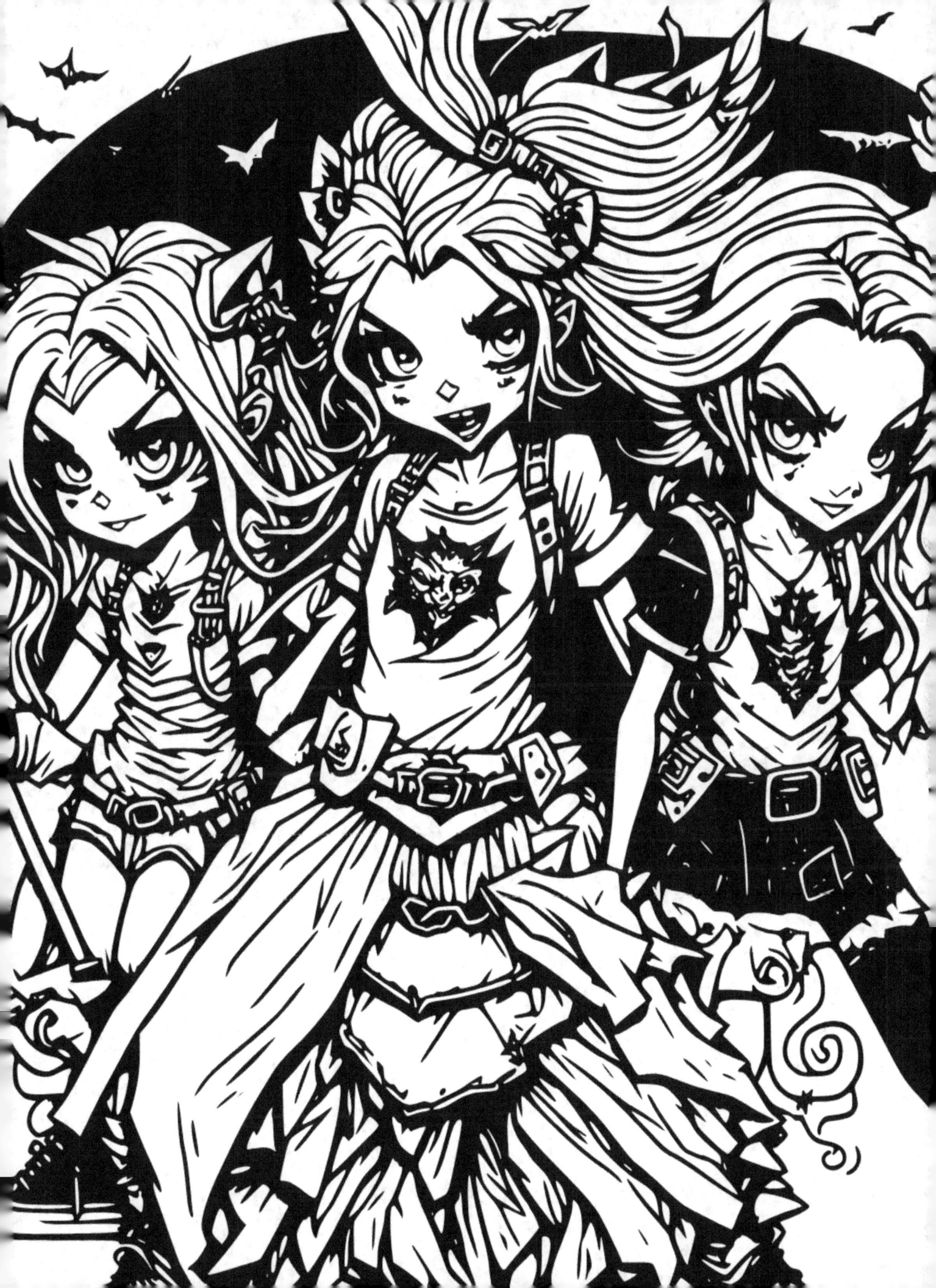

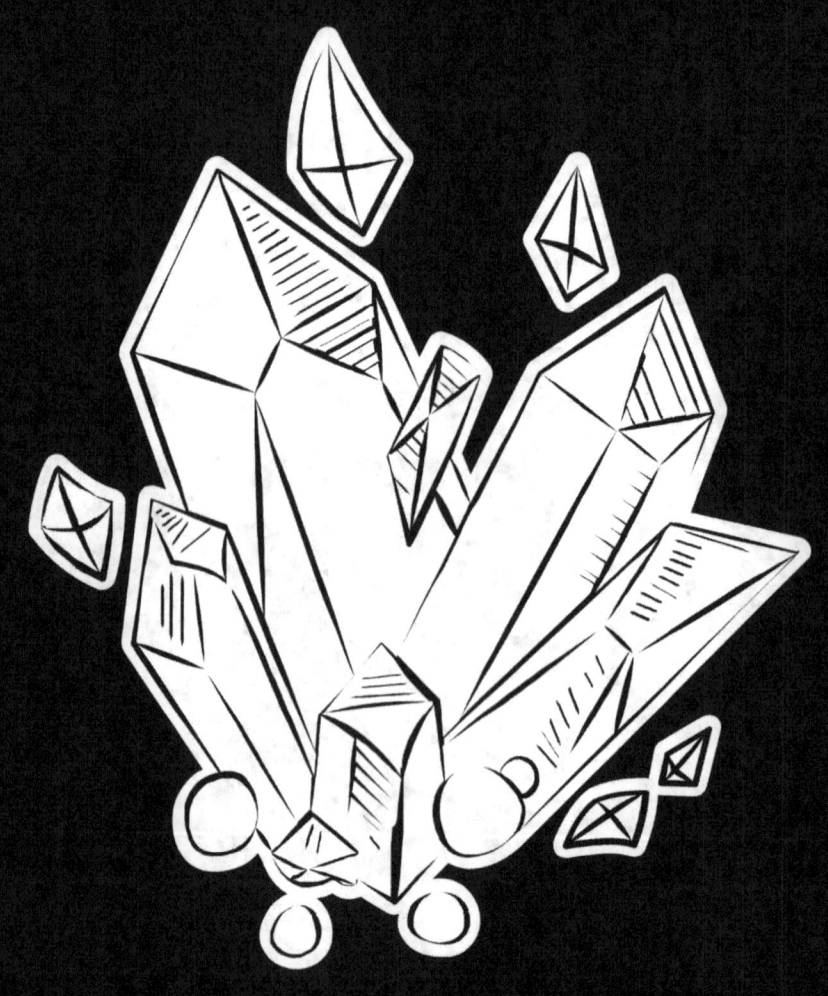

WARLOCKPUBLISHING.COM

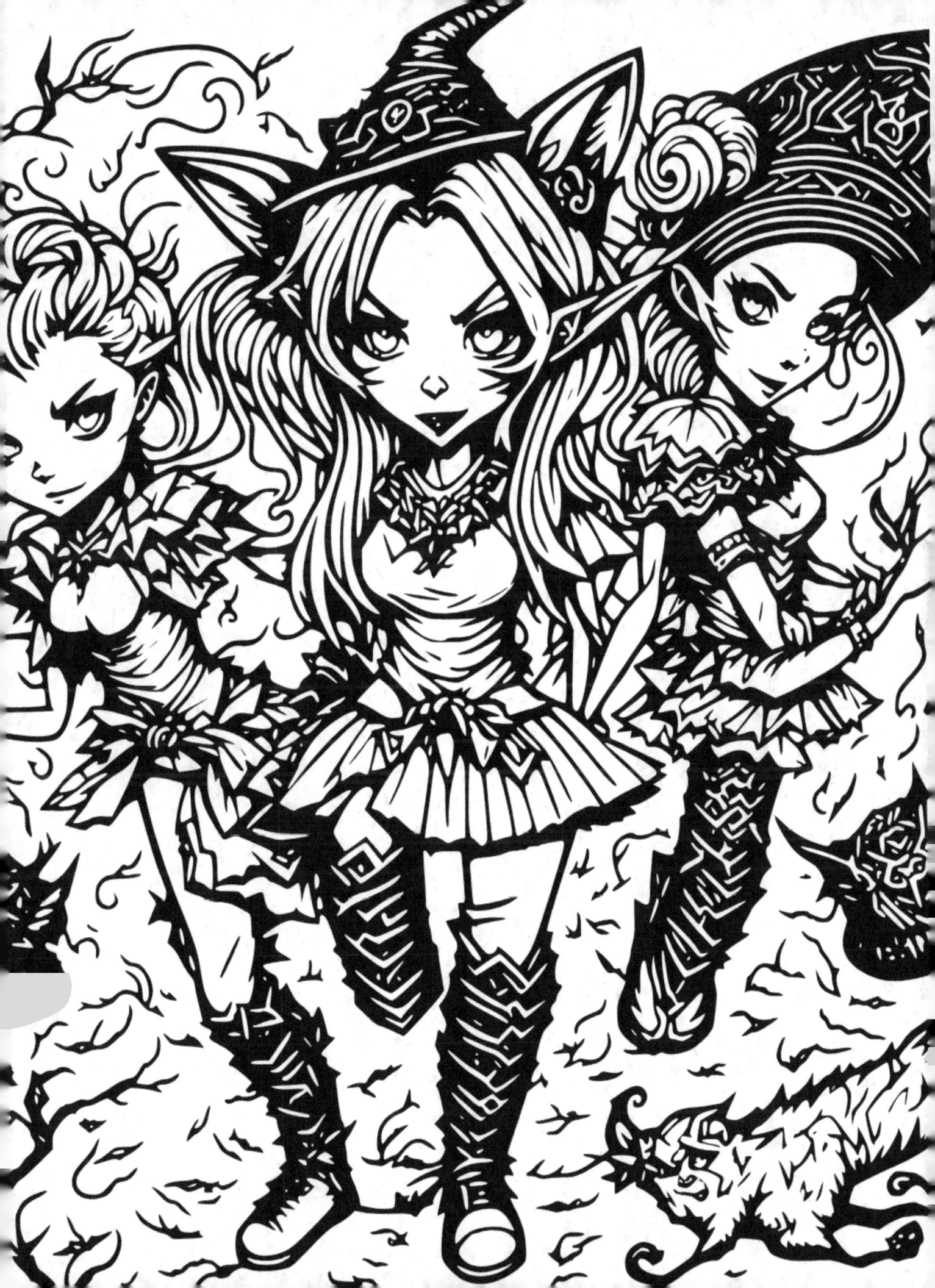

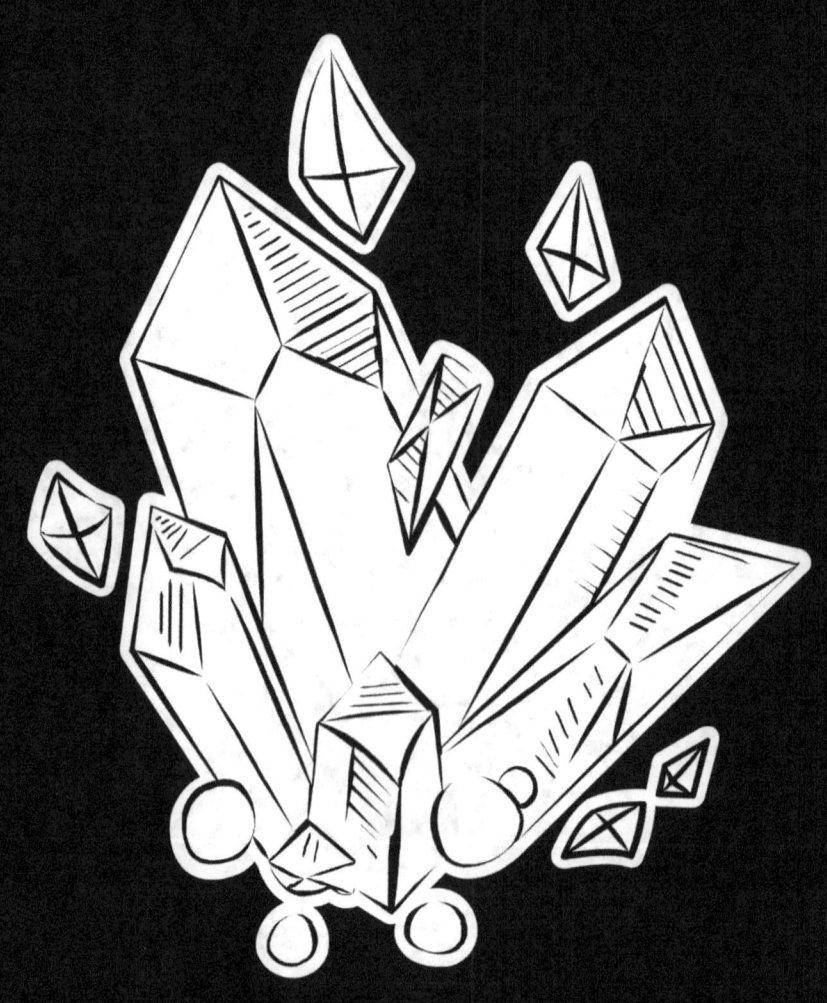

WARLOCKPUBLISHING.COM

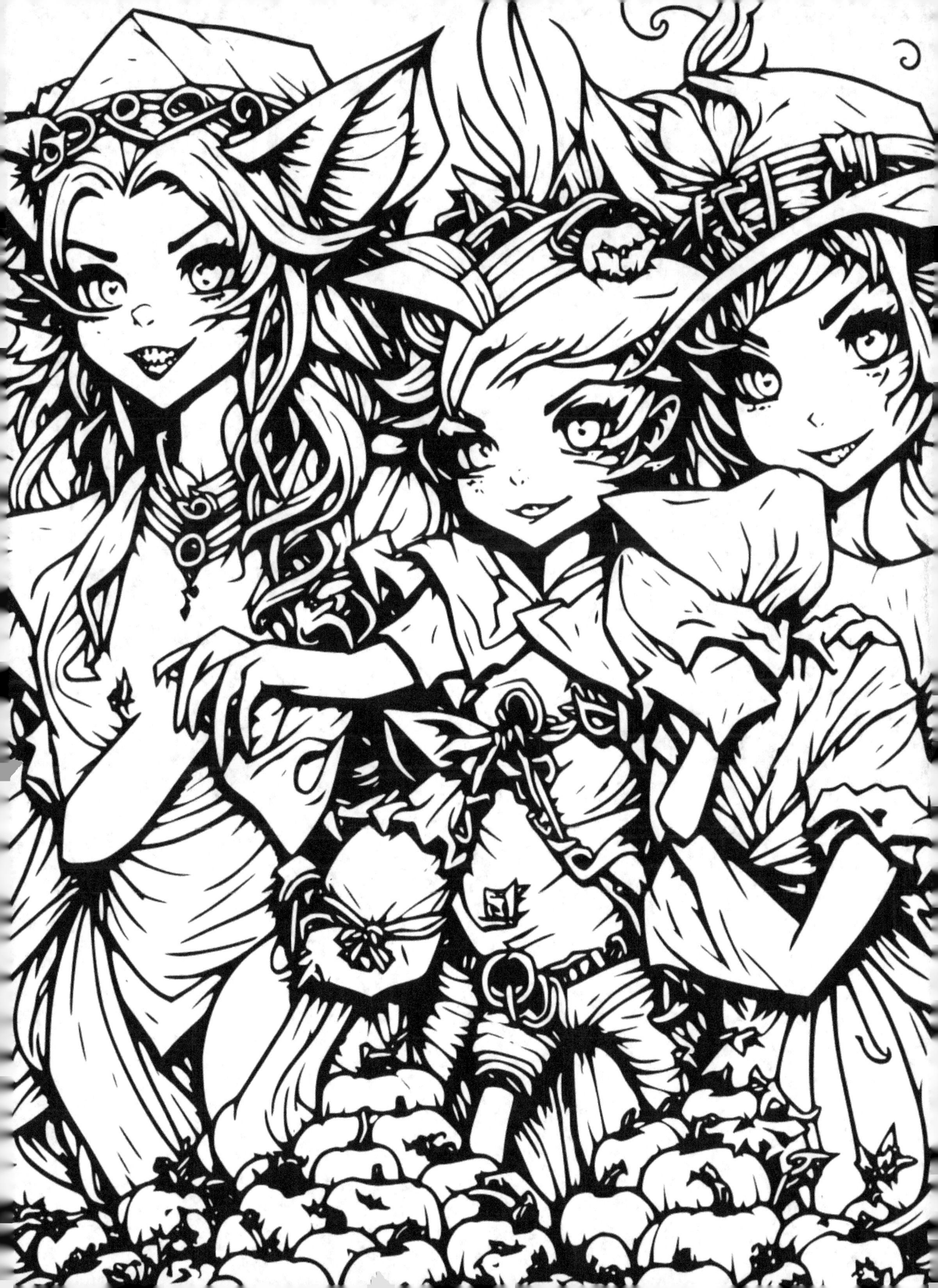

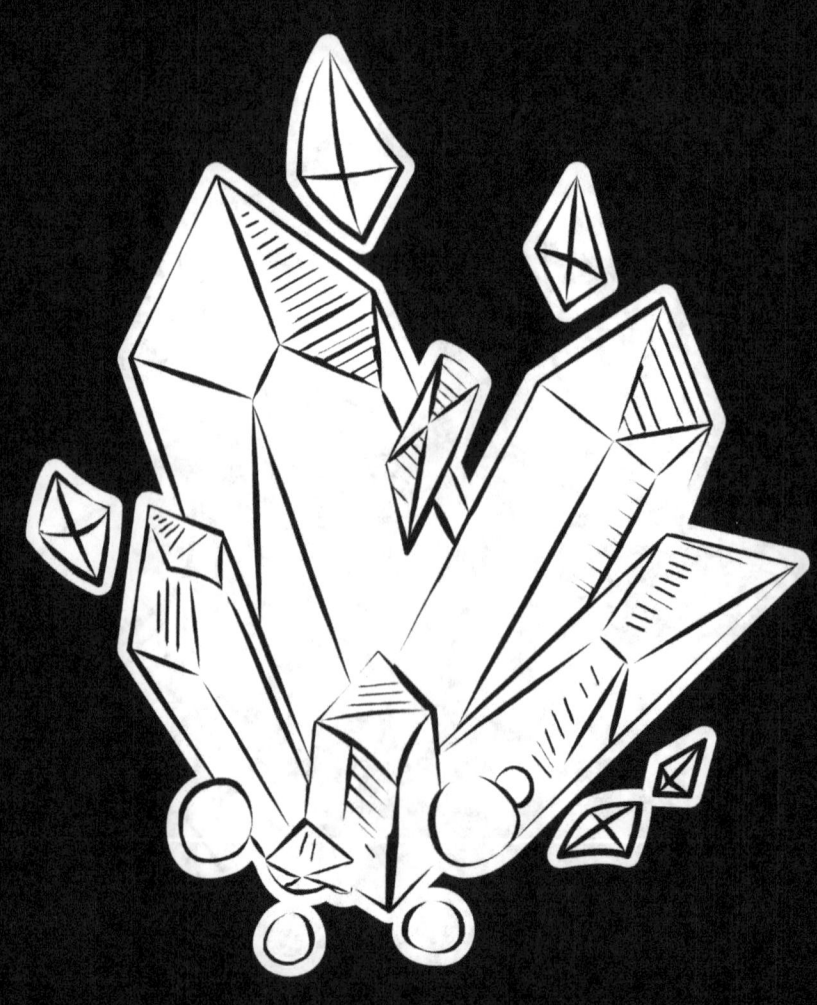

WARLOCKPUBLISHING.COM

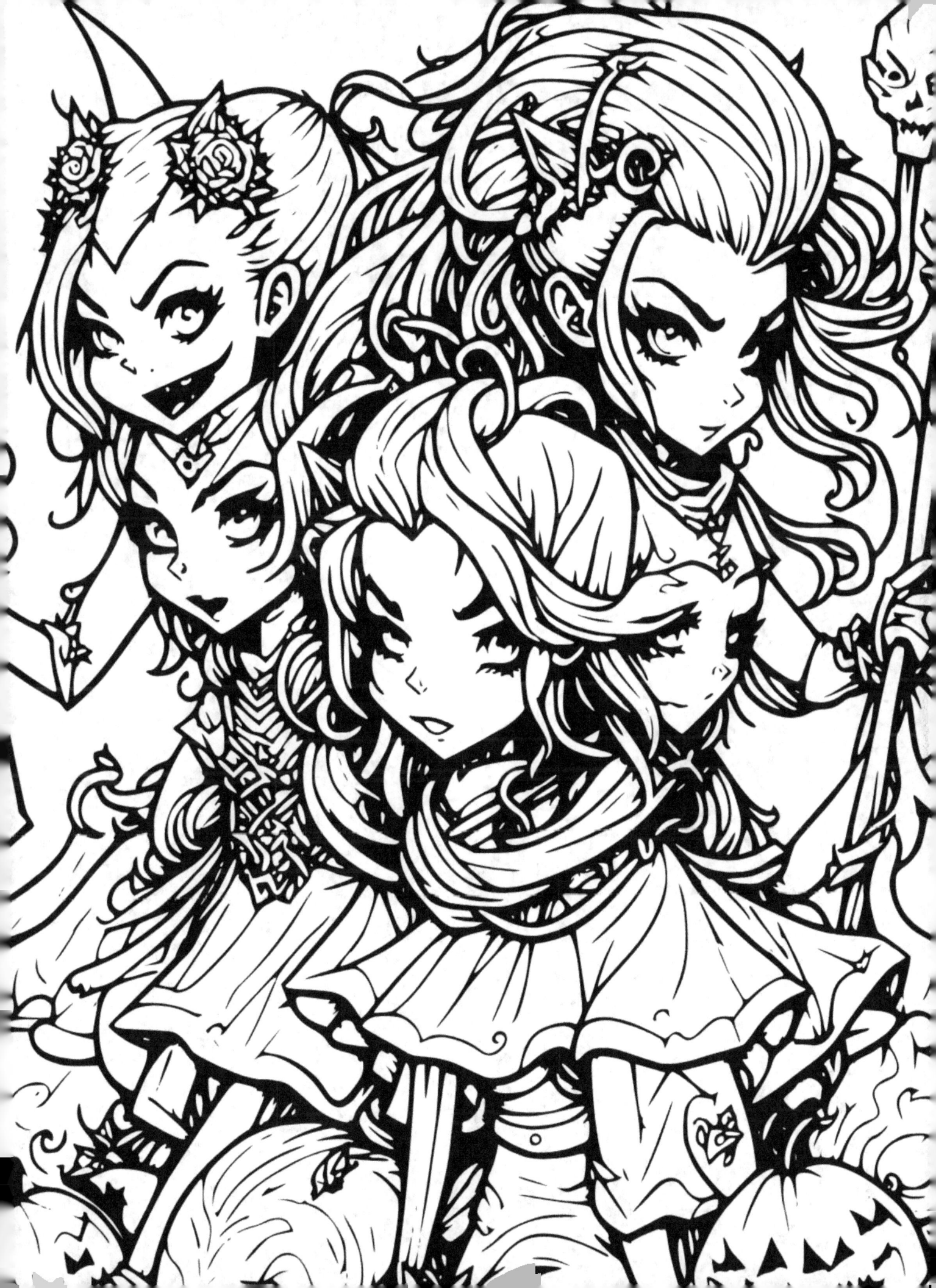

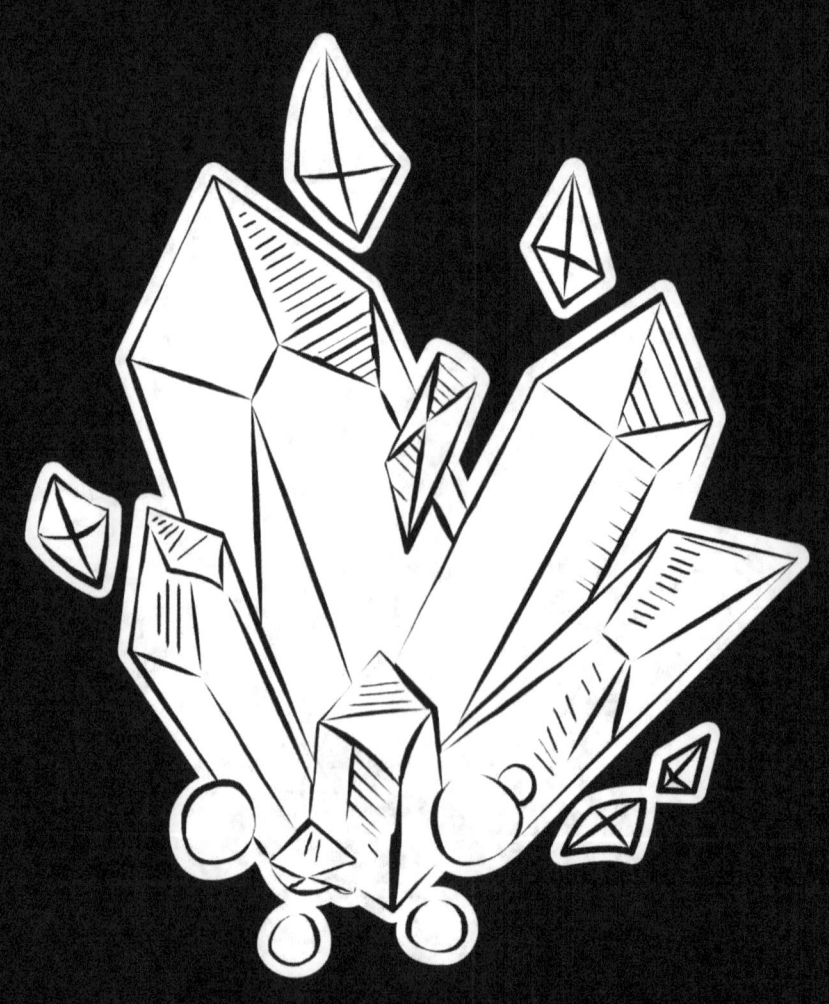

WARLOCKPUBLISHING.COM

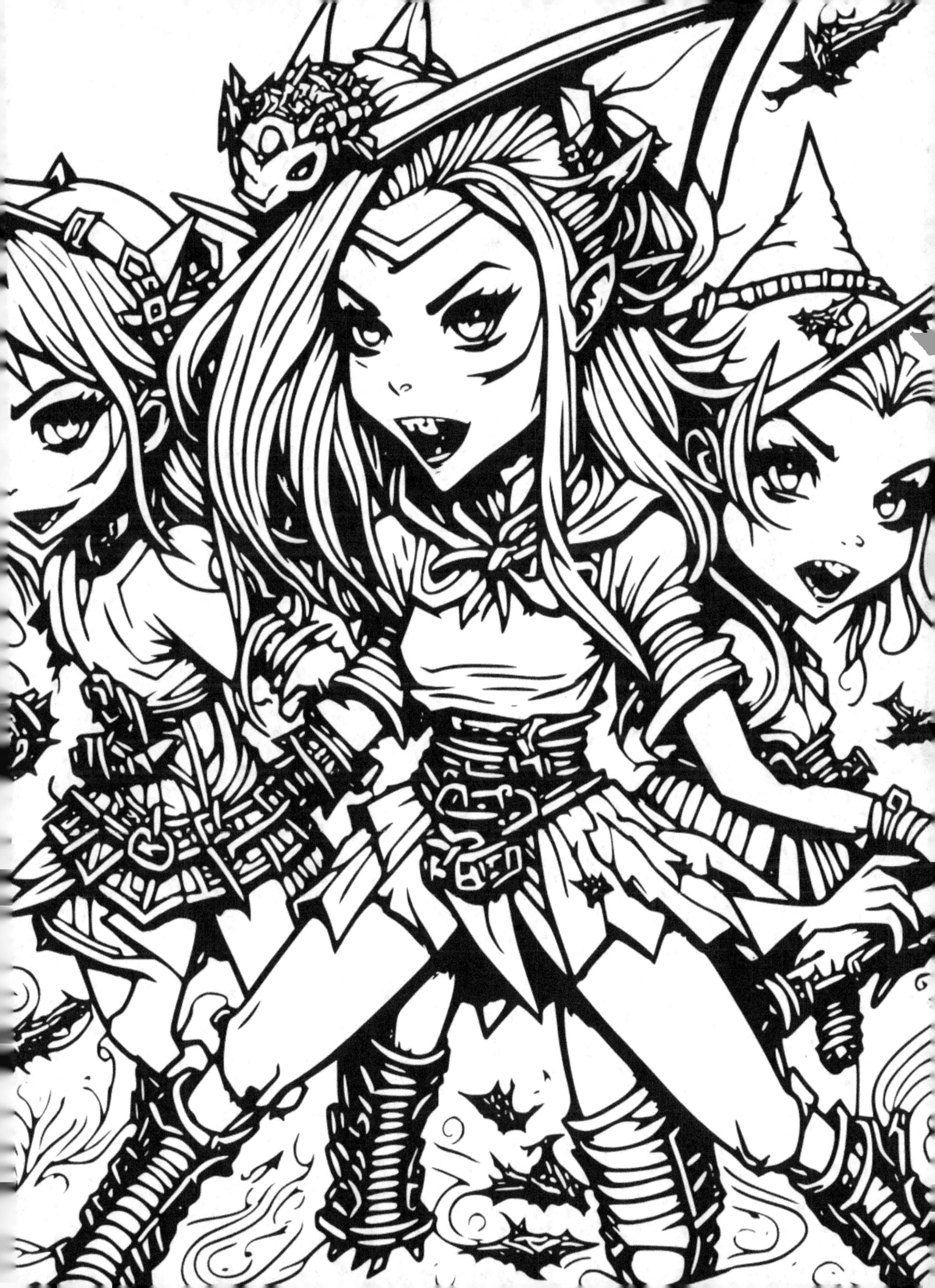

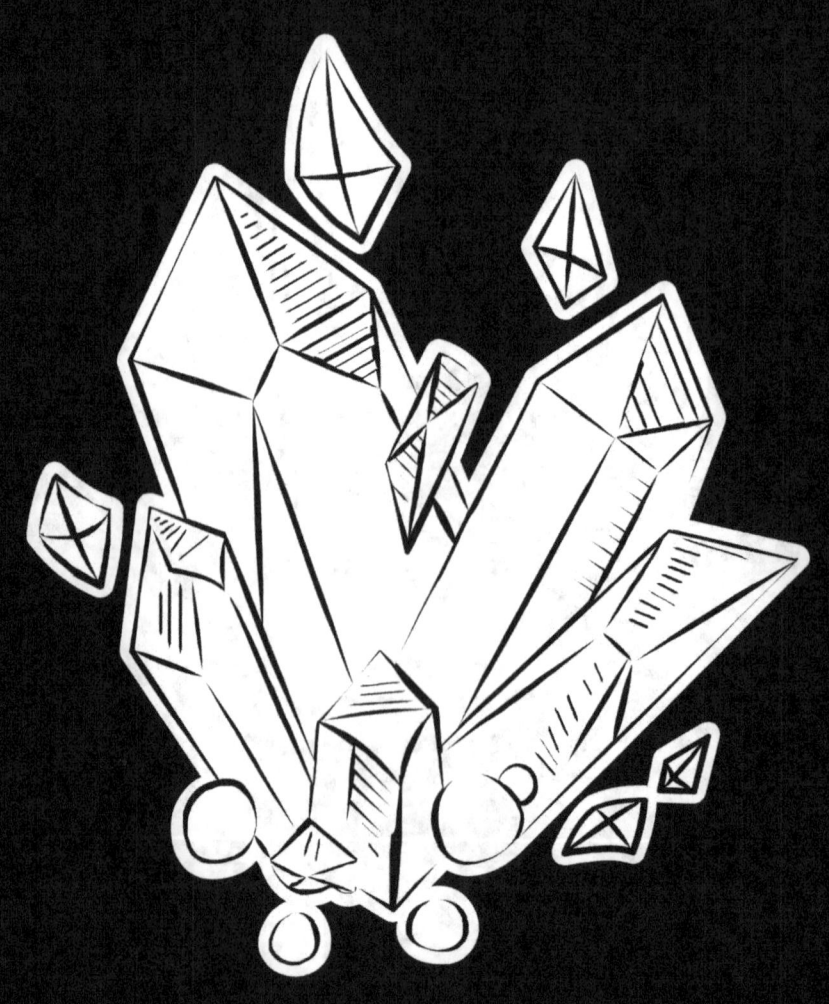

WARLOCKPUBLISHING.COM

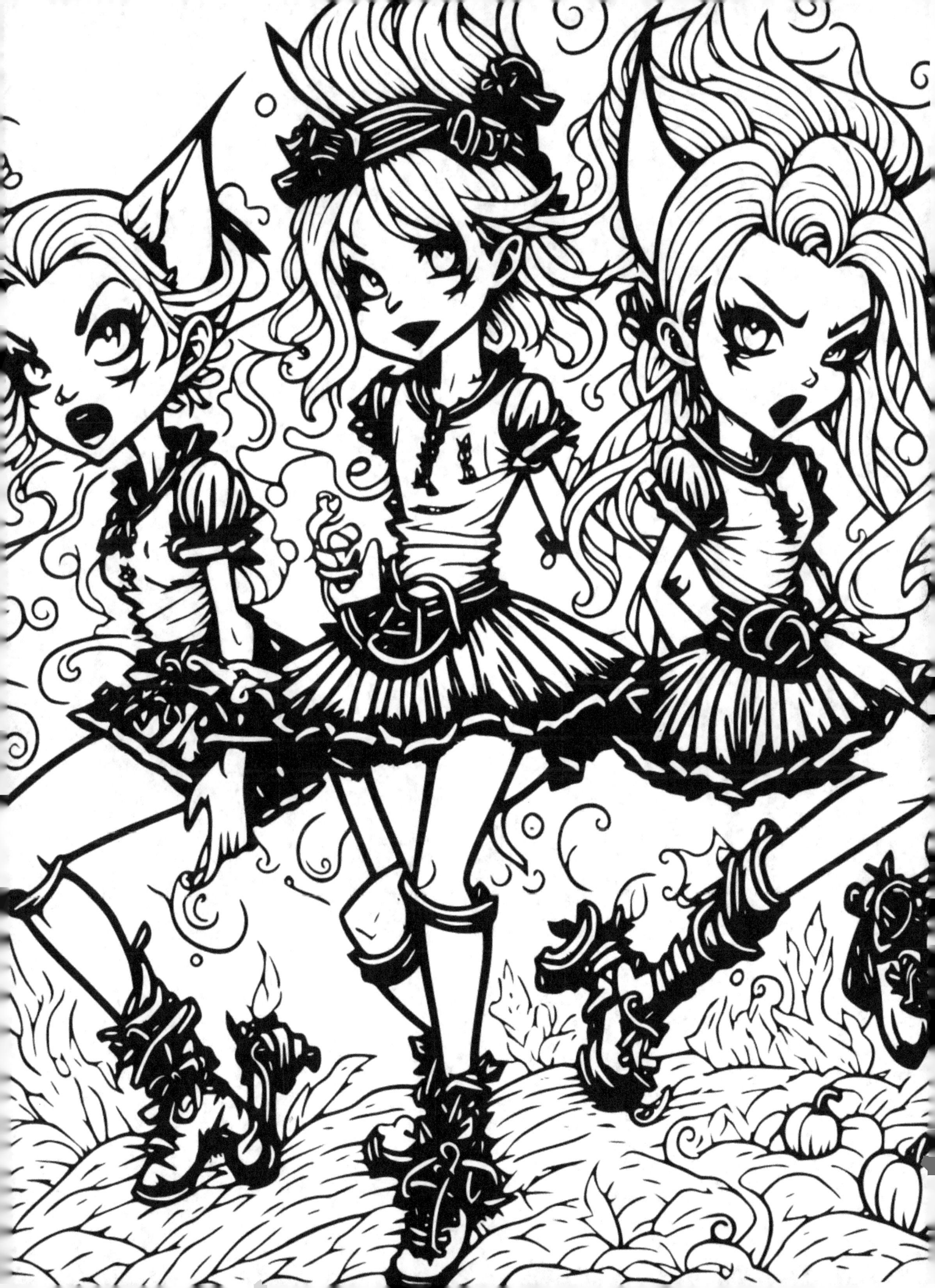

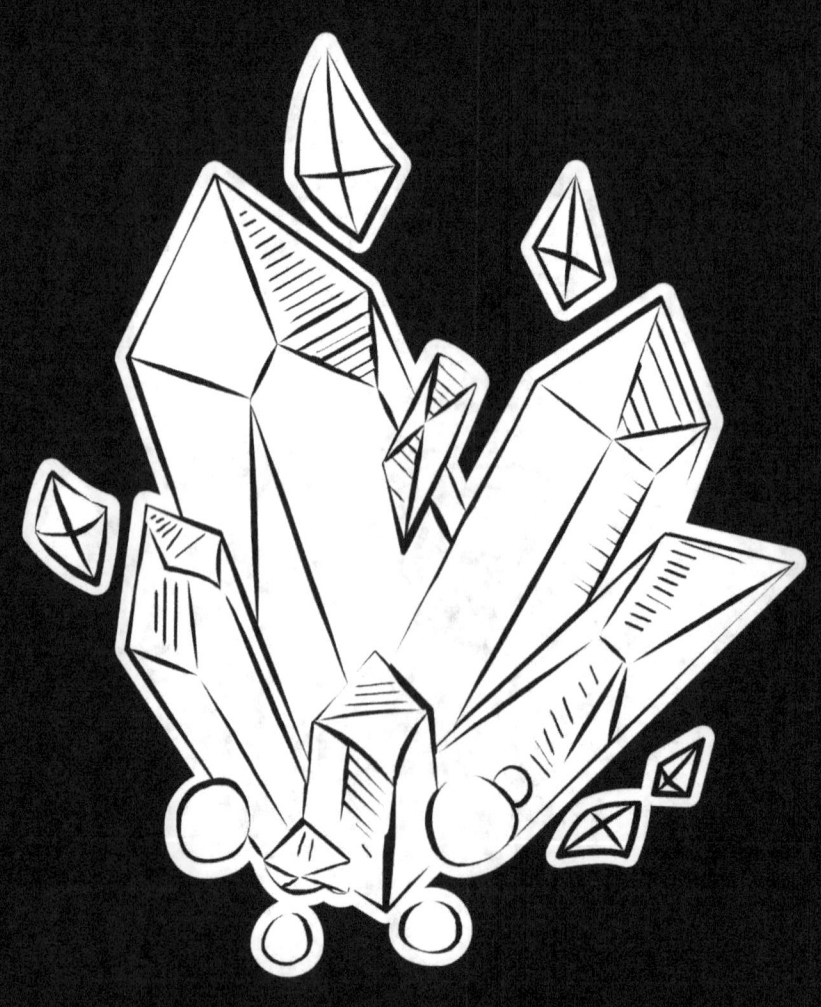

WARLOCKPUBLISHING.COM

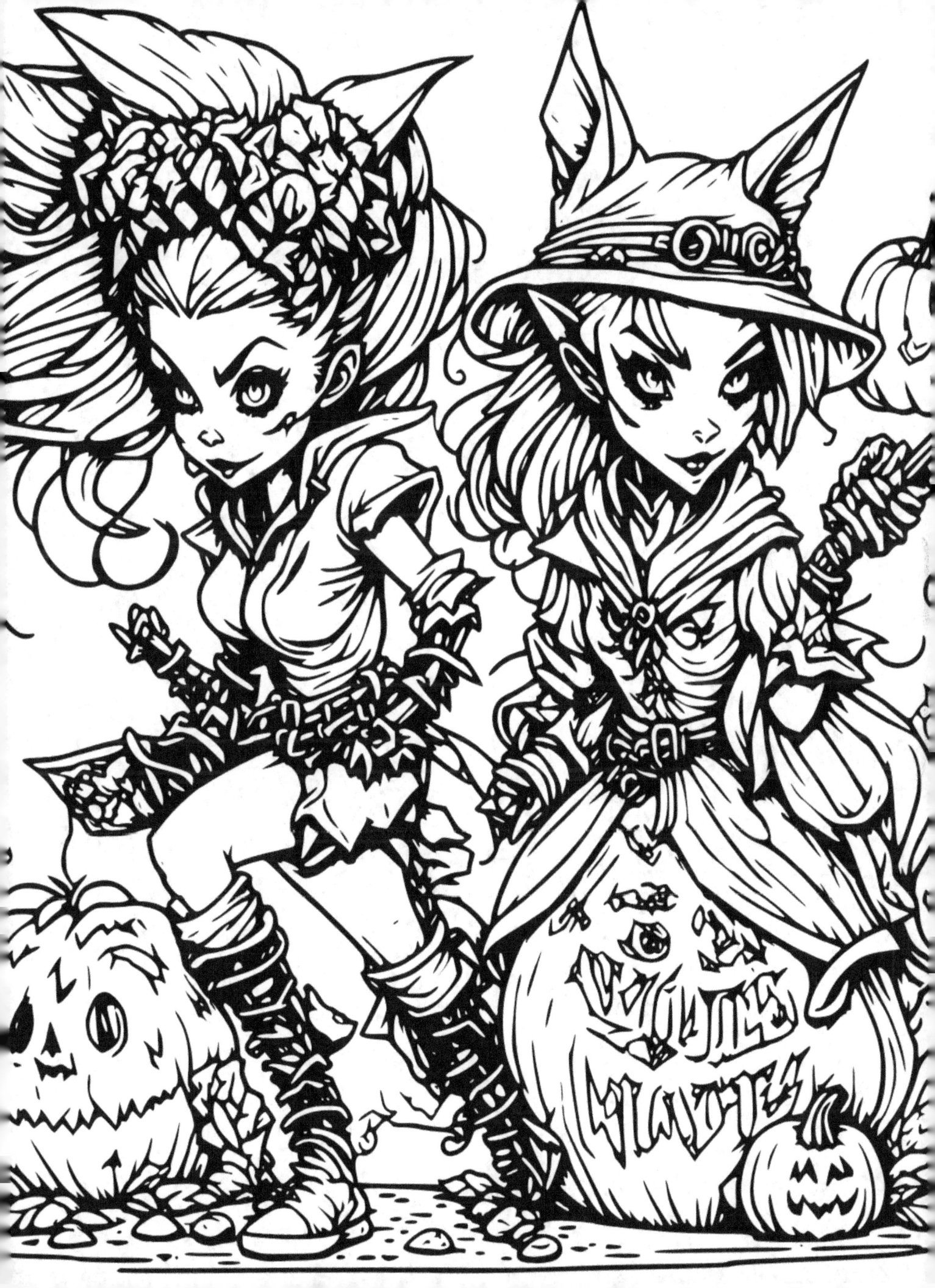

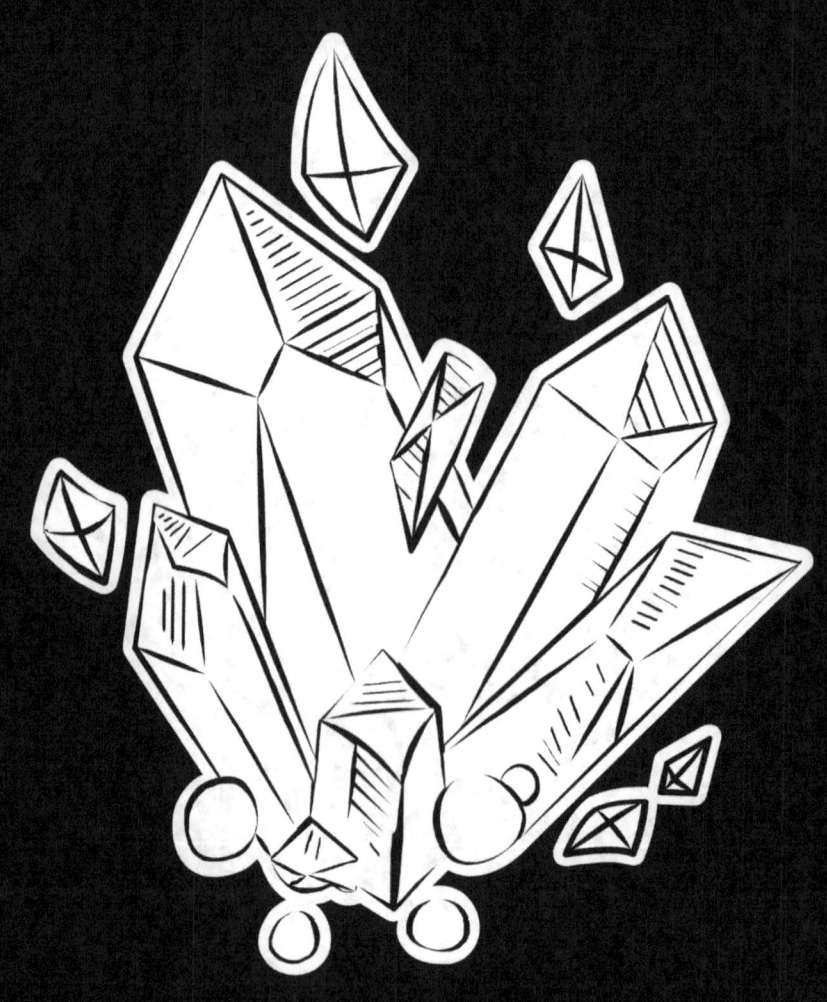

WARLOCKPUBLISHING.COM

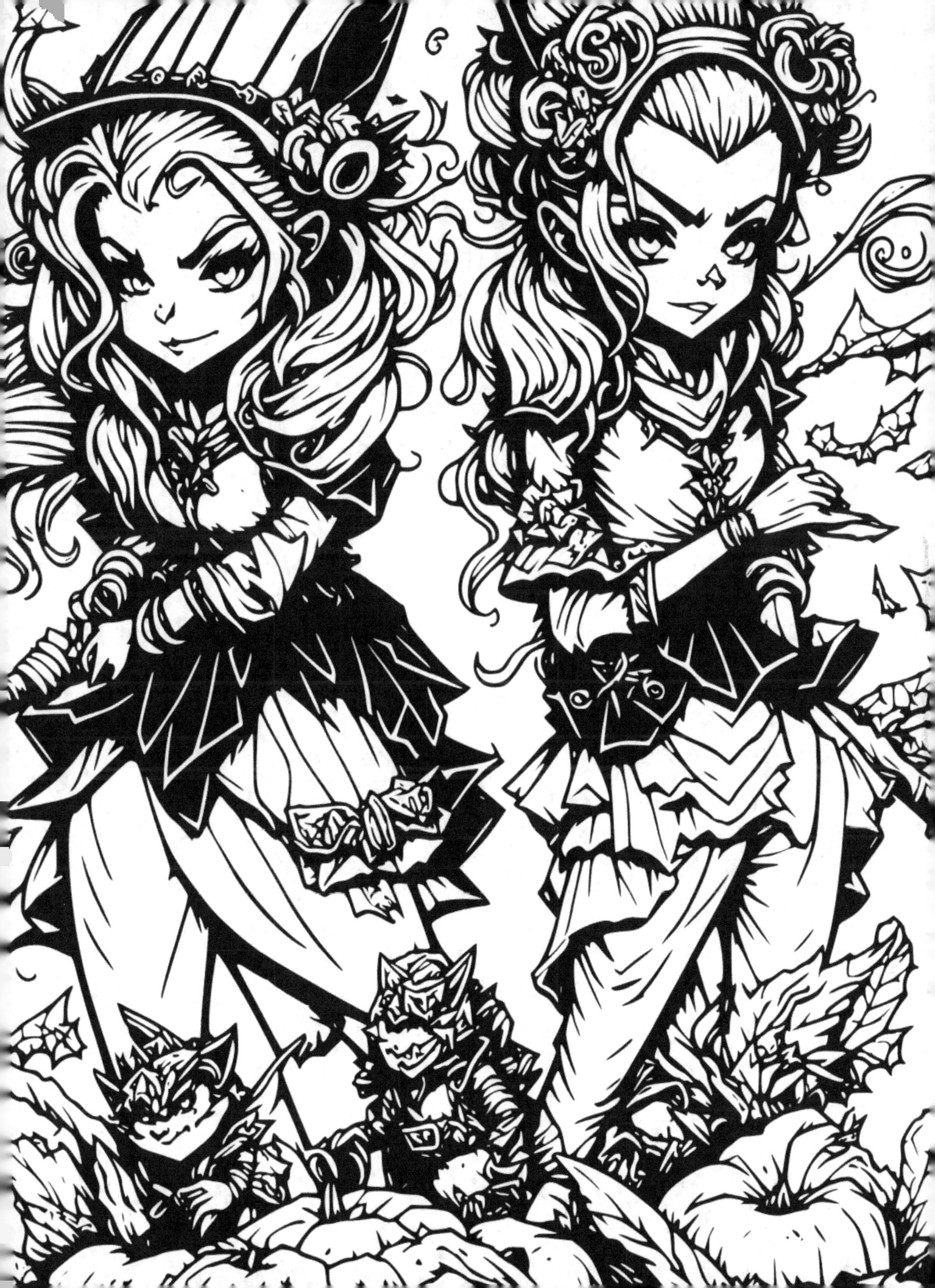

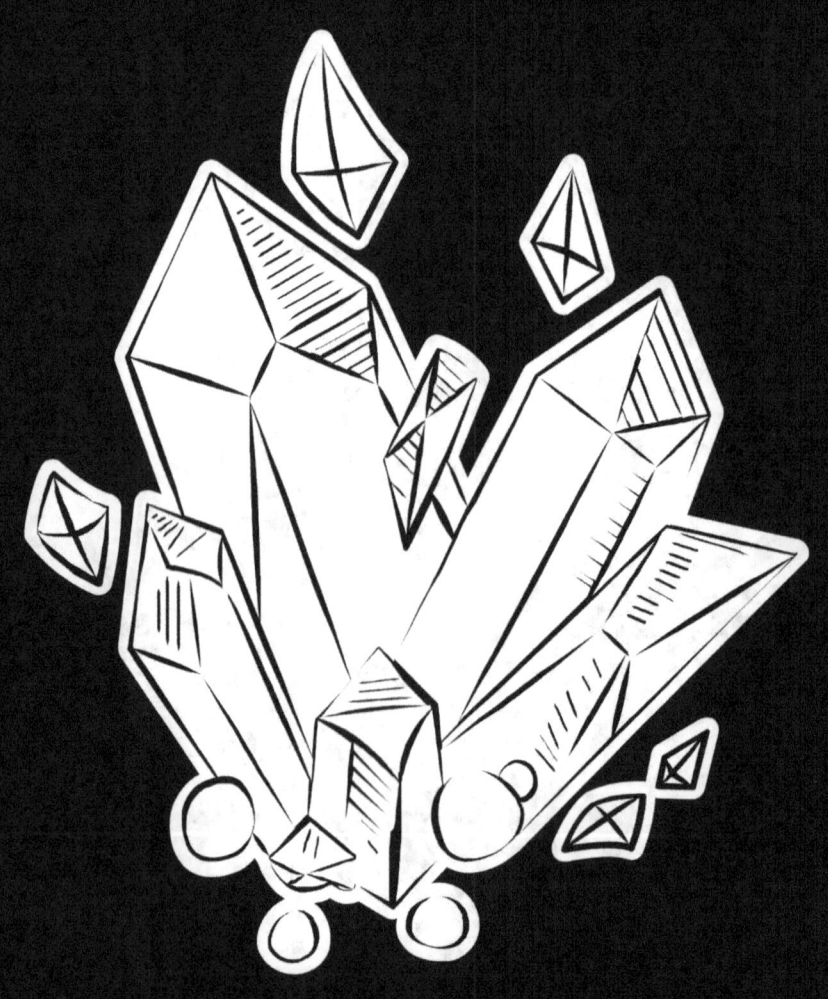

WARLOCKPUBLISHING.COM

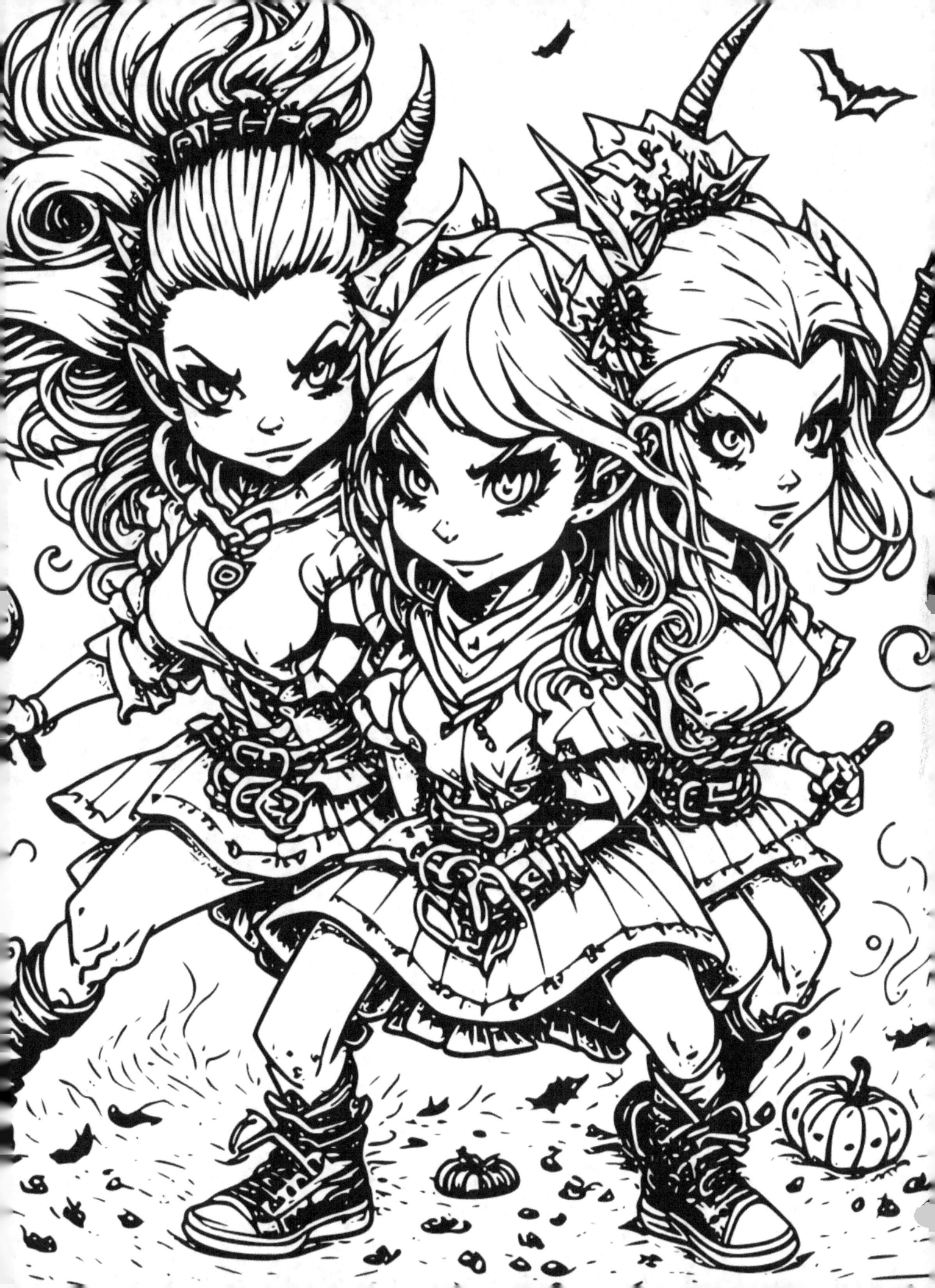

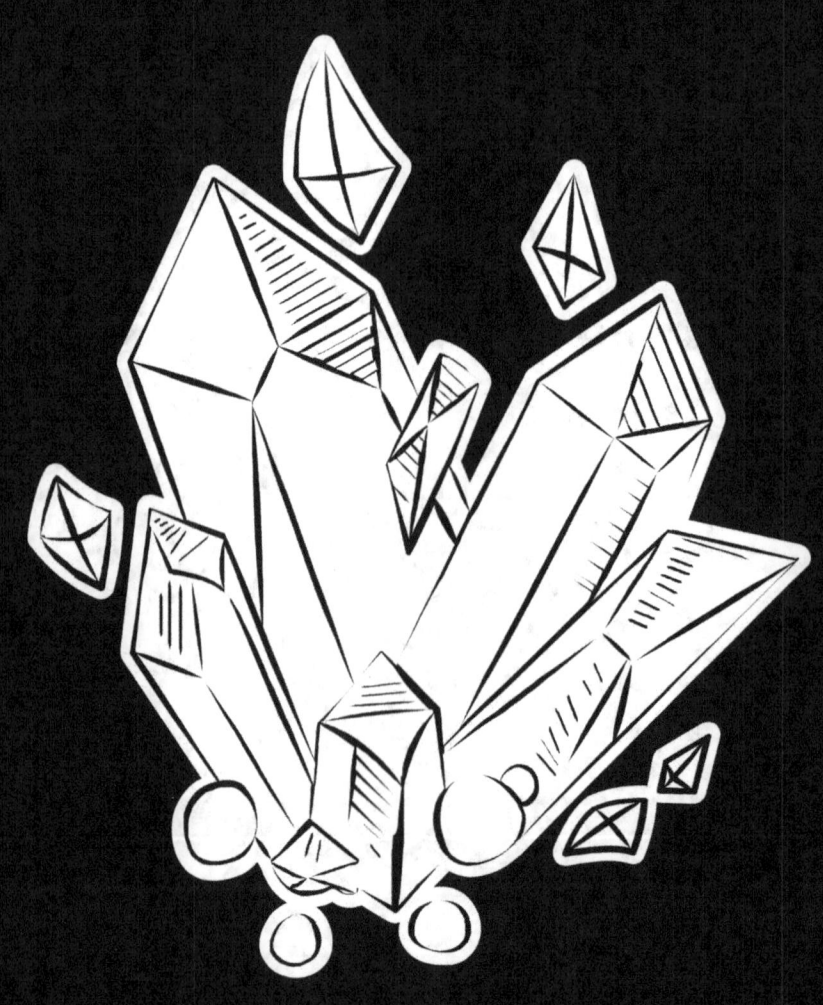

WARLOCKPUBLISHING.COM

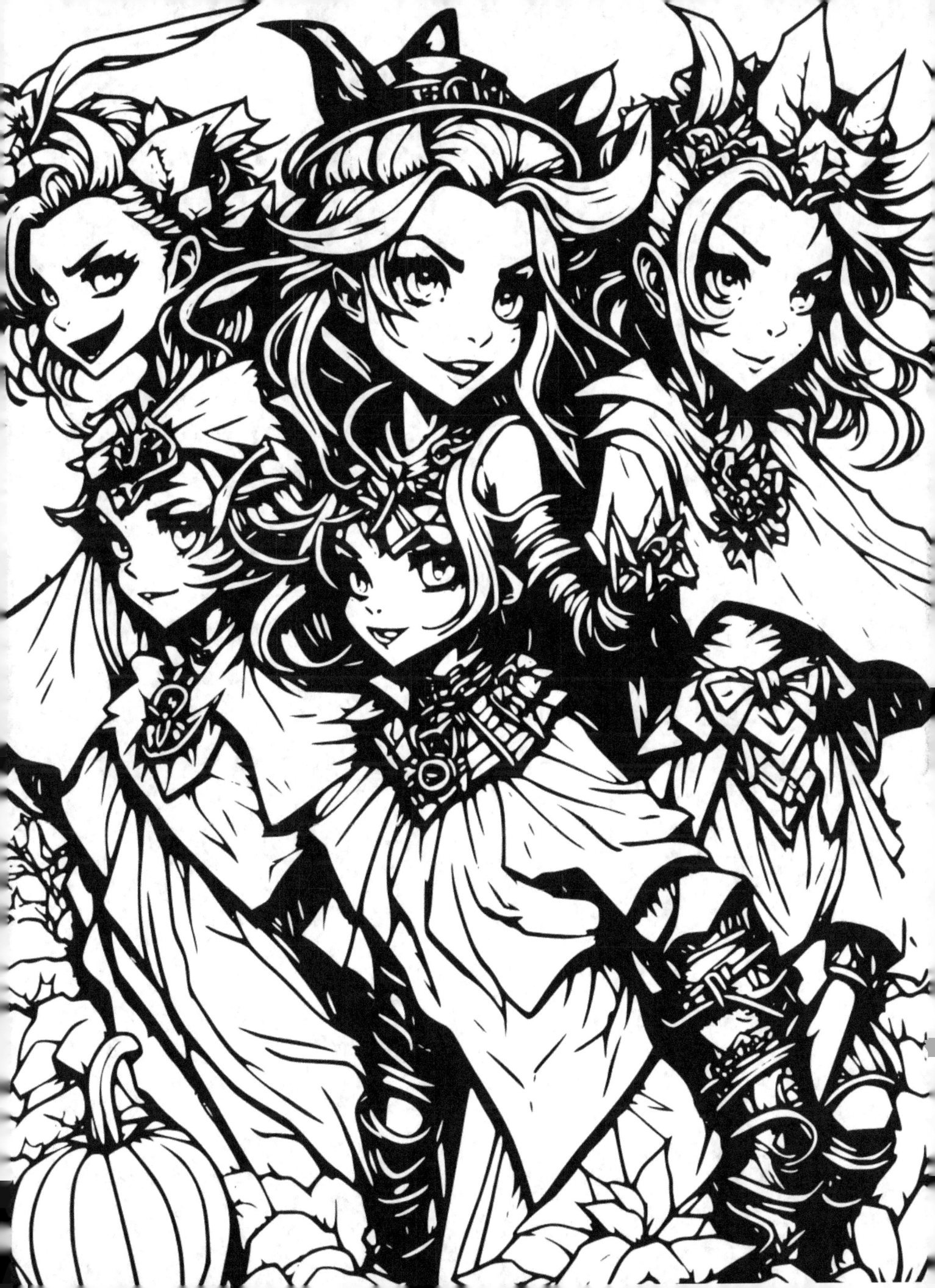

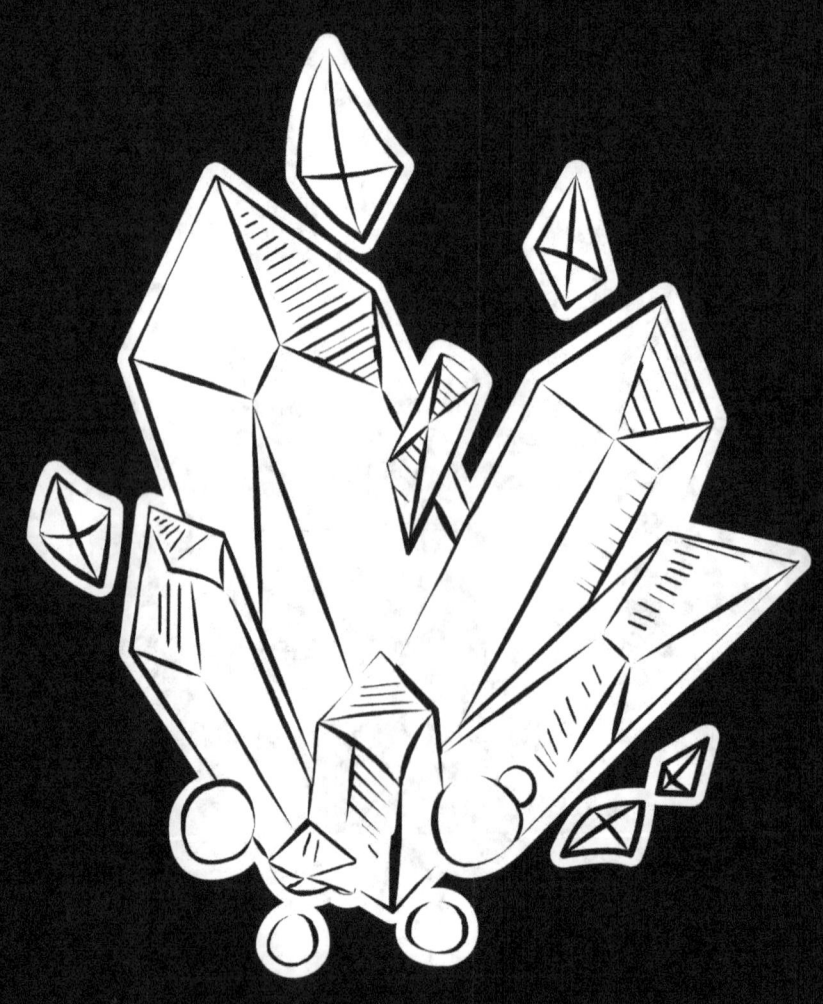

WARLOCKPUBLISHING.COM

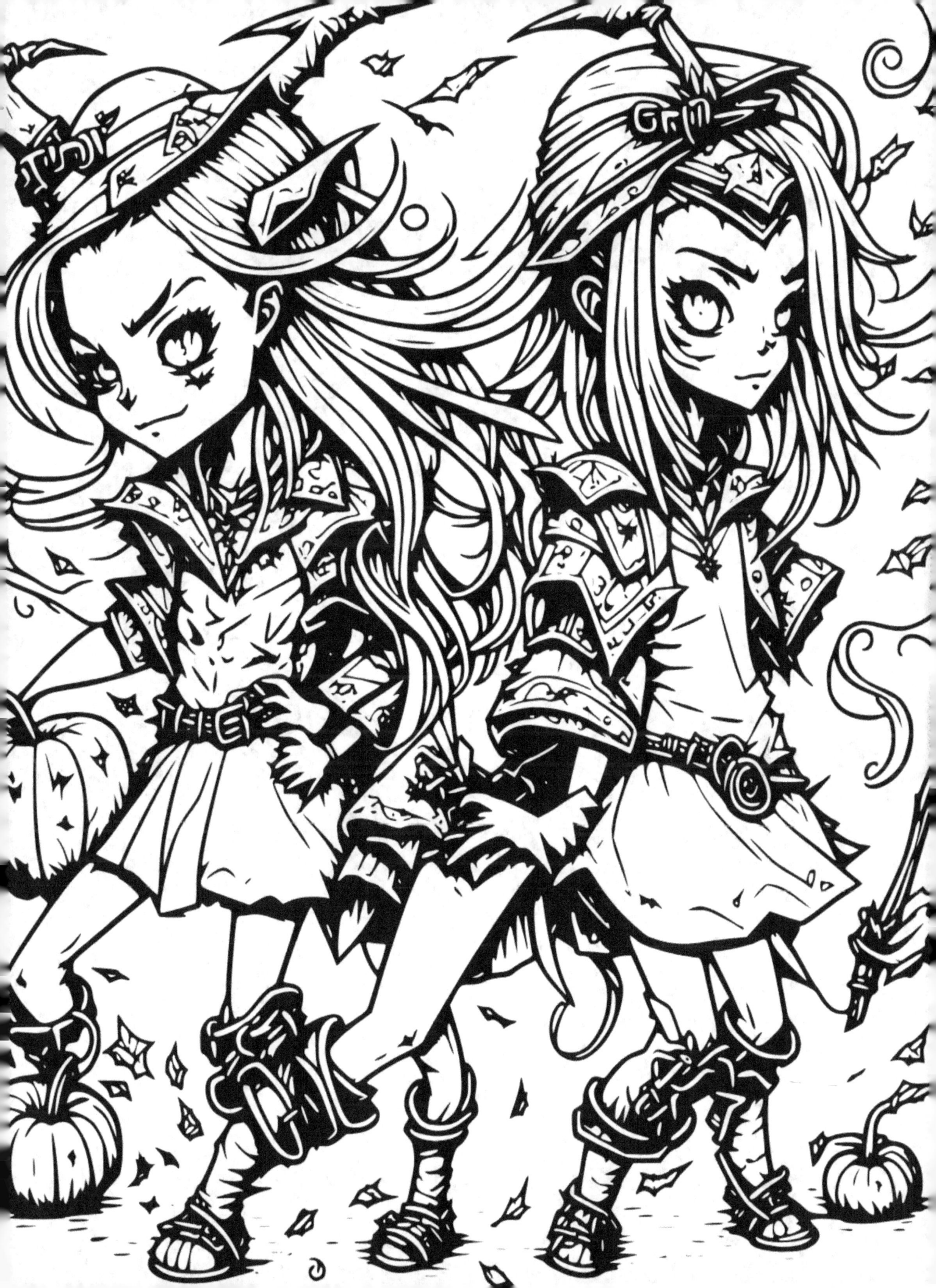

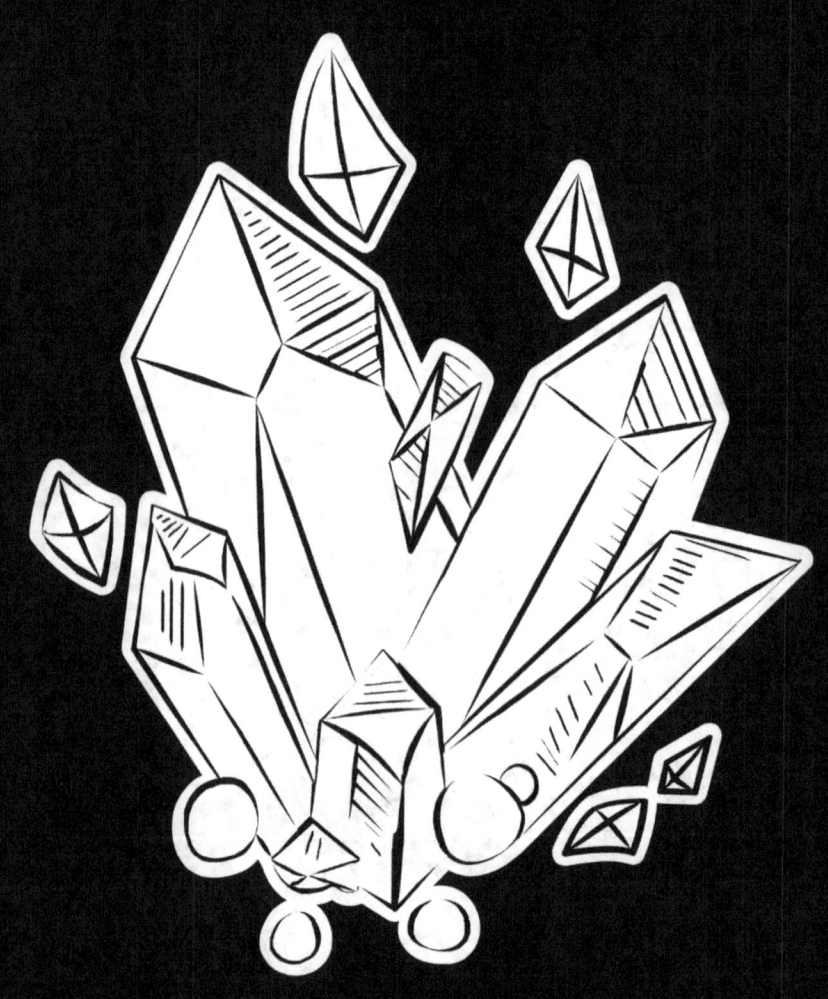

WARLOCKPUBLISHING.COM